Social dialogue and pension reform

United Kingdom, United States,
Germany, Japan, Sweden,
Italy, Spain

Edited by
Emmanuel Reynaud

International Labour Office • Geneva

Reynaud, Emmanuel
Social dialogue and pension reform: United Kingdom, United States, Germany, Japan, Sweden, Italy, Spain
Geneva, International Labour Office, 2000

Pension scheme, social security reform, social pact, Germany, Italy, Japan, Spain, Sweden, UK, USA. 02.04.1
ISBN 92-2-110835-X

Also published in French: *Réforme des retraites et concertation sociale: Royaume-Uni, Etats-Unis, Allemagne, Japon, Suède, Italie, Espagne* (ISBN 92-2-210835-3), Geneva, 1999

ILO Cataloguing in Publication Data

Printed and bound in Great Britain by Biddles Ltd, www.biddles.co.uk

Social dialogue and pension reform

This report was prepared at the request of the Department of Social Security in the French Ministry of Employment and Solidarity, and presented in the context of the mission, "dialogue on pensions", assigned by the Prime Minister to Mr Jean-Michel Charpin, Commissioner-General for Planning.

CONTENTS

Introduction and summary   1

Emmanuel Reynaud*

Pensions today are a major topic of public debate in all the industrialized countries. Systems have been changing everywhere since the early 1980s and will continue to change in the years ahead. Overall, this reflects the combination of a number of factors, in particular schemes reaching maturity, the complete change in the economic and social environment, and changing demographic forecasts. Often described as a "crisis", the process of change is actually inherent in the way national pension systems work, and is a product of the way they are financed, on a pay-as-you-go basis.

All the main public pension schemes, at international level, are financed in this way. Pay-as-you-go financing does not, as is sometimes supposed, consist of paying pensions as they fall due, but involves demographic and economic forecasts, and evaluation and strict control of costs. Pay-as-you-go financing is a technique which has its own tools and methods for achieving schemes that balance over time.

There is a great variety of pay-as-you-go systems around the world. However, whether they pay a flat-rate pension, as in the United Kingdom and Japan, or an earnings-related pension, as in the United States, Germany and Spain, or are even based on cumulative contributions, as in the new schemes introduced in Italy and Sweden, there is no difference from a technical point of view. It is always a matter of balancing resources and expenditure in the long term to ensure the system's sustainability. This approach and the choices involved may be by unilateral decision or through a process involving various forms of consultation, negotiation and public debate. It is the second route that has been preferred in all industrialized countries in recent years, thus illustrating the fundamental basis whereby modern democratic societies make political decisions concerning income distribution.

---

* Chief, Planning, Development and Standards Branch, Social Security Department, ILO.

Despite their significance, the forms of dialogue used and the routes followed by the reform processes are generally not well known. In a way they are the hidden face of recent pension reforms. Most of the work, especially international comparisons, has concentrated on the purely technical aspects: raising the retirement age, changes in methods of calculation and indexation, adjustments to contribution rates and sources of funding, and so on. The decision-making aspects have largely been left in the shadows, yet they are a major factor in the implementation of reforms and the long-term viability of systems.

This report is intended to remedy this lack of knowledge with reference to seven major countries which illustrate well the variety of approaches to pensions: the United Kingdom, the United States, Germany, Japan, Sweden, Italy and Spain. Two of them, Italy and Sweden, are the only examples of industrialized countries which have not merely tinkered with, but have also introduced, a fundamental transformation of the pension system itself. In general, against a background of widely differing institutional environments and traditions, all these countries have introduced consultative bodies and procedures to allow the participation of different actors in developing pensions policy. Thus in each country, parallel to the work of government and the administration, we find all kinds of involvement of employers' and workers' organizations, academics, professionals and experts. It is this aspect – both essential and little known – of the operation of pension schemes and their reform which is studied here.

Each of the seven country studies is structured in the same way. First the general background is covered in a brief outline of the public pension system and the current legislative process. This is followed by a review of the mechanisms and institutional structures involved in the conception and implementation of reforms. Examples of the most recent reforms then illustrate how the process works and how the various actors play their part. Finally, an evaluation highlights the strengths and weaknesses of national social dialogue on the pensions issue.

In this introduction, we summarize the situation in the countries studied, before highlighting the salient points through an overall analysis of the seven national cases.

United Kingdom

It is primarily the Government, in the United Kingdom, that is responsible for drawing up pensions policy. Three official bodies are also involved in the reform process: the Social Security Advisory Committee, the Government Actuary and the Social Security Committee of the House of Commons. In reality, however, these bodies have only a limited influence on the final decision.

The usual practice in pension reform is for the elected government to implement the commitments announced in its election manifesto. A consultation process is then organized on the basis of a Green Paper and/or reports presenting the various options available within the framework of general objectives set out by the Government. These consultations are open to a very wide range of organizations and individuals, but the principal role is in fact played by professionals in the pensions industry, employers' organizations and trade unions, think tanks and, to a lesser extent, pensioners' organizations. Following this period of consultation, the Government presents its proposals in a White Paper, then publishes a bill. At this stage, the opportunities for amending the draft legislation are limited.

In general, the will to achieve a consensus on pensions is very weak in the United Kingdom. The Government uses its majority in Parliament to push its proposals through. Thus, since the 1960s, there has been an "alternating pattern", with bills put forward or introduced by one government being systematically challenged with a change of majority. And during this period, the trade unions invariably backed the Labour Party, while the employers' organizations usually – though not always – supported the Conservative Party's proposals. The question now is whether this alternating pattern will persist in the case of the reforms currently envisaged by the Labour Government.

United States

The United States has a strong tradition of involving representatives of civil society in drawing up pensions policy. In general, two types of institution share responsibility for monitoring the financial development of the public pension system: the Board of Trustees of the system; and periodic social security advisory councils and commissions.

The Board of Trustees consists of four senior civil servants and two private citizens (one a member of the opposition party), who supervise the preparation of detailed projections of the financial status of the pension system. Its annual report gives forecasts of revenue and expenses for the next 75 years. The report is regarded as sufficiently credible to serve as the basis of debates on the financial state of the system and to analyse the impact of proposed reforms.

The social security advisory councils and commissions have traditionally played a very important role. With members representing a wide range of political interests, their purpose, in parallel to the legislative process, is to arrive at a consensus on the pace and direction of reform. Since 1937,[1] almost all major changes to the public pension system were adopted only after a broadly representative advisory council or commission had considered them and made recommendations. Since the 1960s, the arrangement had been formalized and put on a regular footing. Every four years, the Government had to appoint a new advisory council to examine all aspects of the system. The approach was abandoned in 1995, with the creation of a permanent advisory council.

The system worked well until recently. The last periodic advisory council, which published its report in early 1996, was not able to reach a consensus on the measures needed to take account of the ageing of the population. A deep "philosophical gulf" opened up between those who wanted to adapt the existing system to the new situation and those who wanted to replace it, in whole or in part, by privately administered personal pension plans. The gap between the two groups is such that it is unlikely that a consensus will be found in the near future.

Germany

Participation by the social partners is integral to the German public pension system, the statutory pension insurance. This is organized on a self-managed or self-administered basis (*Selbstverwaltung*); in other words, the institutions which manage the system have boards made up of representatives of employers and the insured. The law also provides for the involvement of the Social Advisory Council (*Sozialbeirat*).

The Social Advisory Council, introduced as part of the 1957 pension reform, consists of 12 members representing the insured (four representatives), employers (also four), the Federal Bank (one) and the economic and social sciences (three). It is responsible, in particular, for giving an opinion on the Government's annual report on pension insurance. This report and the accompanying opinion are mainly concerned with the financial management of the system. Since 1997, they must also indicate the possible implications of raising the retirement age for the labour market, the financial situation of pension insurance and other public budgets. The Social Advisory Council is also routinely involved in debating and adopting laws to reform the pension system.

The Social Advisory Council is part of a network of various contacts and multiple forms of cooperation between the social partners and the Government. The network ranges from ad hoc expert committees to round tables organized under the Federal Chancellery. In general, the social partners in Germany are to a large extent involved in decisions on pension issues, often alongside academics and representatives of other groups such as the churches.

This approach, which consists of involving various social groups in formulating pensions policy and seeking a fairly broad consensus, for a long time proved its worth. The last reform, however, was passed in 1997 amid great controversy, and the new Federal Government, which came to power at the end of 1998, has re-opened the debate on the measures previously adopted. This is a first in the field in the Federal Republic.

Japan

In Japan, the law requires a regular review of the pension system at least once every five years. This is one of the highly original features of the pension situation in Japan. The last reform was in 1994 and a new reform was prepared for adoption in 1999.

The process of review and reform is mainly performed by the Pensions Office (*nenkin kyoku*) in the Ministry of Health and Social Affairs. It normally takes two years and follows a timetable that is repeated from one reform to another. It begins with the creation of a Pensions Advisory Committee (*nenkin shingikai*) composed of representatives of the civil service, academics and civil society (in the shape of employers' organizations and trade unions). The idea is that the officials in charge of the review can consult the users; but the former nevertheless retain a considerable degree of control over the process, and in particular produce the final report. Based on this report, and in close liaison with the ruling party, the Liberal Democratic Party (LDP), the Pensions Office drafts a bill for debate in Parliament. The preparation of the 1999 reform also contained an innovation: the publication in May 1998, on the British model, of a White Paper, in which the Pensions Office set out its views separately from the Pensions Advisory Committee.

In general, Japan has a permanent mechanism for steering the pension system with the five-yearly "rendezvous" imposed by law. It has also put in place a formal consultation process which involves experts and social partners in the decision-making process. Nevertheless, discussion of pension issues remains limited and largely controlled by the administration and the governing party, the LPD. Given the party's currently weaker political position, and a bill that proposes reduced benefits and increased contributions, the 1999 reform can be expected to give rise to a more lively debate than is usually the case.

Sweden

Sweden has just introduced a major change in its public pension system. It is in the process of moving from a two-tier system, with a basic flat-rate pension and a supplementary earnings-related pension, to a single defined contribution system.

Before the reform was adopted, the Swedish pension system was the subject of thorough debate over 20 years. Various parliamentary and government commissions, in particular, considered the various issues at stake. The process which led to the

5

current reform was itself formally launched in 1984 with the creation by the Government of a special commission. This was composed of members and experts representing all the political parties in Parliament, the main employers' organizations and trade unions, and social groups particularly affected by pensions. After several years' work, it submitted its final report in 1990 with a proposal for reform of the pension system. The reactions were such that the Government preferred not to proceed in that direction and decided to form a new commission composed of all the political parties in Parliament. It was this commission which, in March 1994, proposed a wholesale reconstruction of the system. The proposal was supported by the four parties in the Government and the main opposition party, the Social Democratic Party. On the basis of this proposal, the Government set out the general principles of the reform which were adopted by Parliament in June 1994.

A working group was then set up from the parties represented in Parliament, and in favour of the reform, to translate the general principles into a draft law. At the same time, a debate within the Social Democratic Party (which returned to power in September 1994), in which opposition had arisen to some aspects of the bill, led to new negotiations between the five parties that supported the reform. It was finally in the spring of 1998 that the proposal for the new system was presented to Parliament, which adopted it in June 1998. The first pensions under the new system will be paid in 2001.

The pursuit of a consensus was a characteristic feature of the Swedish approach. However, from the point of view of the actors involved, a change occurred during the long process of preparing the reform. It began with a vast study involving the social partners and other groups. Later, those concerned were essentially the political parties represented in Parliament and, in the last stage, the reform only involved the political parties which supported it.

Italy

Italy, like Sweden, has fundamentally changed its public pension system. Of the industrialized countries, these two countries are in fact the only examples of large-scale reforms in recent years. Italy is in the process of moving from a system in which pensions were earnings-related to one based on contributions paid. It was also decided to harmonize the many existing schemes with the general system for private sector employees, which became the reference model for the whole pension system.

The process which led to the Dini reform in 1995 had several stages. First, a long period of debate during the 1980s did not produce a decision, although most of the actors recognized the need to make structural changes. Then emergency adjustment measures were taken following the devaluation of the lira and Italy's exit from the European Monetary System (EMS) in 1992. These measures included highly disadvantageous provisions on pension levels in the long term, without solving the structural problems and inconsistencies in the system. In 1994, the Government set up an expert commission whose members were nominated by the Government itself, employers' organizations and trade unions. The commission failed to reconcile the different views expressed by its members. Despite trade union opposition, the Government decided to go ahead and introduce in the autumn of 1994 a series of pension measures in its finance bill. The scale of the reactions were such that it had to pull back, and that probably contributed to its downfall.

The Dini Government, which followed, took a totally different approach. It entered into direct negotiations with the main trade unions and associations of the self-employed and with the employers' organizations. Trade union representatives, in particular, were informally involved at every stage of the drafting of the Government's bill. This "dialogue" resulted, in May 1995, in an agreement between all the economic and social representatives, except for the main employers' organization. The Government, in particular, made the concession of a long period of transition from the old to the new system, and the trade unions, for their part, undertook to persuade their members of the need to change the old system, even though it was more favourable. The Government's bill incorporating the terms of the agreement was put before Parliament and adopted in August 1995 with only a few minor amendments.

The Italian model of social dialogue involved giving responsibility to the social partners, especially the trade unions. The approach was crowned with success because it led to a radical reform of the pension system in 1995. However, its limitations were revealed two years later when the Government wanted to revise the agreement concluded in 1995. The results of the negotiations this time were very limited. The trade unions found it difficult to accept the proposed new reforms aimed at stabilizing expenditure, especially as a member of the ruling majority in Parliament, the *Rifondazione Comunista*, was against it. It is probable that had there been a broader consensus, the difficulties would have been overcome.

Spain

In the mid-1990s, Spain adopted an approach of seeking consensus on pensions. Prior to that, pensions had been a potential source of high tension, especially between the Government and the trade unions. In 1985, for example, a law to reform the pension system led to the first national strike since the restoration of democracy. The subsequent government measures led to a one-day general strike in December 1988.

Faced with the worrying state of the pension system and the difficulties encountered in reforming it, Parliament decided to set up a working group made up of representatives of all the parliamentary groups. The work of the group led, a year later, in February 1995, to the conclusion of a political accord between all the parties, known as the "Toledo Pact". The aim was to consolidate the existing pension system and prevent it from becoming a political pawn between the parties, especially at election time. This political accord was extended in October 1996 by a socio-political "consolidation agreement" between the Head of the Government and the general-secretaries of two major trade union confederations. The employers, who had reservations about the financial viability of the Toledo Pact, did not wish to associate themselves with the measure.

The general principles contained in the Toledo Pact and the consolidation agreement were translated into a law on "the consolidation and rationalization of social security", which was passed in July 1997. It introduced important new provisions such as the separation of sources of financing (since contributions now covered only contributory benefits and the State became responsible for the non-contributory ones), the creation of a reserve fund and greater linking of pension levels to contributions paid. It is an example of a negotiated legislative instrument to the extent that, having been formally debated and adopted by Parliament, it was the subject of extensive discussion, first among the political parties, and then between the Government and the trade unions. The measure, finally, made it possible to make the changes necessary to ensure the sustainability of the system without engendering conflict.

**

Apart from the differences, several common features emerge from the analysis of the decision-making process relating to pensions in the seven countries studied. Before considering them, we need to clarify an important point concerning international comparisons. The purpose is not to import ready-made solutions from abroad to solve problems faced at domestic level. There is often a great temptation to adopt such an approach, but it inevitably leads to a dead end. National pension systems are the product of the societies concerned and inevitably reflect a series of specific characteristics, especially concerning the relationship between the State and society, political traditions, industrial relations, structure of the economy, and perceptions of justice and equality. If the analysis is to have any meaning, it is crucial always to relocate national structures and experience in their general context. International comparisons can then be extremely useful. By opening a window on different realities, they are one of the best ways of achieving a better awareness and understanding of one's national situation. They can also help in developing and introducing new ideas and original solutions, appropriate to the particular context.

The comparative analysis of the seven country studies shows several common features, from which useful lessons applicable to public pension systems in general can be drawn.

First, the examples studied show the importance of having credible technical data, meaning data that are both reliable and accepted by the various actors, concerning the financial state of pension systems and prospects for the future. These data are the basis for discussion and debate, and can lead to informed political choices from among the available options. The institutional forms corresponding to this technical awareness vary from country to country. In the United Kingdom, it may be an independent institution within the government structure (the Government Actuary); in the United States, the Social Security Administration (on which the opposition party must be represented) is responsible for financial monitoring; in Germany, the figures are produced by institutions whose reputation guarantees their validity (Federation of Pension Insurance Institutions, Federal Office of Statistics, Federal Bank). The formulas vary depending on the country, but the important point is that the data concerned are available and that their credibility is beyond question.

In addition, there is in all the countries a trend towards establishing advisory bodies or working groups to participate, permanently or on an ad hoc basis, in the decision-making process relating to pensions. In countries such as Germany, the United States and Japan, advisory councils are an integral part of the process of monitoring and periodic review of the system. Their composition is fairly similar. In particular, they include representatives of employers' organizations and trade unions, academics and qualified experts. In a complex and highly technical area such as pensions, these councils are forums for examining the system and reaching a compromise to assist decision-making by legislators. In Sweden and Spain, for example, parliamentary working groups played a major role in the reform process, by allowing the formation of a consensus on a topic of potential conflict. In general, parallel to the institutional mechanisms, the pensions debate is everywhere driven in a variety of ways: creation of ad hoc commissions, production of reports and White Papers, or organization of symposia by the political authority. As a rule, it is largely outside the usual institutional framework.

Overall, most countries, on the pensions issue, show a marked will to find a consensus between the different political and social forces. Pensions are a special area in the context of the representative democracies. They involve a clash between two types of logic: on the one hand, the logic of very long-term commitments (50, 60, 70 years, or even more), which require guaranteed sustainability and, on the other, the logic of alternating policies typical of parliamentary democracy. In the case of pensions, therefore, there is often a concern for continuity that goes beyond partisan politics, as well as the adoption of practices which can be termed "exceptional" in relation to the decision-making process. In Sweden, for example, the change in Parliament in 1994 from a liberal-conservative to a social-democrat majority did not seriously affect the process of reform. The composition of the parliamentary working group responsible for drafting the bill did not significantly change. In Spain, all the parliamentary groups decided in 1995 to conclude a pact on the pensions issue and remove it from the election debates. The Government then negotiated with the trade unions before presenting a bill to Parliament. In Italy, the Government takes the same approach, consisting of negotiating the contents of the reform directly with the trade unions and incorporating the terms of the agreement in the bill.

In this area, where the will to achieve a consensus and continuity is predominant, one country – the United Kingdom – constitutes an exception among the seven countries studied. The alternation between Conservative and Labour administrations has regularly led to major changes in pensions policy, which raises the question of trust in the sustainability of the commitments given and the overall coherence of the system.

By taking a historical perspective, it can also be concluded that the pursuit of compromise on the pensions issue was easier in the past because it came in a period of strong economic growth and the maturing process of the systems. Today the situation is tighter in that the arbitration needed to achieve a balance in the long term between pension system resources and expenditure involves difficult choices. The opening of dialogue in making these choices, given the difficulty of the task, is all the more necessary.

Notes

[1] The public pension system was established in the United States in 1935.

The structure of pension reform in the United Kingdom

2

Bryn Davies•

Introduction

This country study describes the institutional structure and practice of pension reform in the United Kingdom. The purpose is to describe the British experience relating to the mechanisms employed to monitor the development of the public social security pension system and to achieve a consensus in finding the balance between needs and resources.

The study is in six sections, as follows:

- an outline of the British pension system and an explanation of the terminology which is used to describe it;
- an explanation of the legislative process through which the pension system is established and changed;
- a description of the formal structures that exist for the review and development of pension provisions;
- a description of how pension provisions are reviewed in practice and the roles of the main actors in that process;
- an account of how the process functioned in the most recently completed set of pension reforms and how it has been developed in the context of the further reforms that are currently under consideration; and
- some observations on the strengths and weaknesses of the system.

The terms of reference for the study refer only to the "public social security pension system". It is important to understand, however, that in the United Kingdom part of the public system is effectively delivered through private pension arrangements. How this works is outlined in the following section, but the important consequence is that the distinction between state and private

* Director, Union Pension Services, London.

pension arrangements is not as clear-cut as in many other countries. It is therefore necessary for this study to deal to some extent with mechanisms for the reform of private as well as state pensions.

Outline of the public pension system

In the United Kingdom the term "social security" refers to the whole system of compulsory social protection, including unemployment and sickness benefits as well as pensions, which provides workers who have paid the necessary contributions with benefit entitlements as of right. The system is still known formally as "national insurance" (NI).

The pension element of the National Insurance Scheme has two components. First, there is the flat-rate component, generally referred to as the state basic pension. This is paid to all working people providing they have had earnings in excess of the lower limit for NI contribution purposes and hence have paid NI contributions, or have been given contribution credits during periods of unemployment, sickness, and so on.

The second component, paid in addition to the basic pension, is the additional pension, or the State-Earnings-Related Pension Scheme (now generally known as SERPS), which, as the name suggests, is linked to earnings. SERPS began operation in 1978 and although the value of its prospective benefits was reduced through further legislation in 1986 and 1995, its structure remains as it was when first established. The benefit is a percentage of the individual's average revalued lifetime earnings between the upper and lower earnings limits for NI contribution purposes (25 per cent for those retiring at present but falling to 20 per cent in coming years).

SERPS is provided automatically for all employees paying NI contributions apart from those in "contracted-out" pension arrangements. The principle underlying this system of contracting out is that employees with private pension arrangements that have been approved as meeting certain standards can give up their entitlement to SERPS benefits and, in return, they and their employers pay lower rates of NI contributions. The general requirement for approved arrangements is that they should be expected to provide benefits that are as good as or better than those that would have been provided by SERPS. Such arrangements can be occupational pension schemes, i.e. a group arrangement sponsored by an employer or individual personal pensions taken out through insurance companies or similar institutions.

Both components of the NI pension are funded on a pay-as-you-go basis, where current NI contributions are used to fund current benefits. Although notionally there is a "national insurance fund" it is, in practice, simply an accounting fiction in the national accounts. The income and expenditure of the fund are brought into balance each year through adjustments in the contribution rates or by making payments into or from general revenues. The management of the fund and its administration, involving such matters as the maintenance of records and the payment of benefits, are functions of central government departments with no involvement of the contributors or the social partners.

The legislative process

The main provisions of the National Insurance Scheme are set out in primary legislation (Acts of Parliament), with detailed arrangements laid down in secondary legislation (statutory instruments).

Acts of Parliament are the result of a full legislative process repeated in each of the Houses of Parliament, the House of Commons and the House of Lords. The process starts with the proposed instrument, known as a "bill", being formally presented to one or other House by the Government in what is known as the "first reading". It then goes through consideration in principle, known as the "second reading"; consideration in detail, normally by a committee of members and known as the "committee stage"; a report back to the full House by the committee, known as the "report stage"; and a final review by the full House, known as the "third reading". Amendments to the bill can be made at any stage except the first and second readings. The entire process is then repeated in the other House, with the added complication that if amendments are made by the second House they have to be referred back to the House that first considered the bill for its agreement. When both Houses of Parliament have agreed on the provisions of the bill, it receives formal consent and becomes an Act.

Secondary legislation also requires approval by both Houses of Parliament, but through a much simpler process. In this case draft statutory regulations, made under the provisions of an Act of Parliament, are presented to each House. In most cases they automatically become law within a defined period unless either House votes against their acceptance, although some more important regulations require a formal vote in favour by both Houses.

The content and the timing of legislative proposals are in the hands of the Government. Although there are provisions whereby individual members of either House can introduce legislative proposals, the procedures that have to be followed mean that there is little or no chance of their success. However, members of either House can move amendments to government bills at the appropriate stages, although this is mainly the role of the spokespersons for the opposition parties rather than individual members acting on their own. In any event, amendments to a bill cannot divert the proposed legislation from its main objectives. There is no facility for outside bodies or individuals to have any input to the legislative process other than by lobbying the legislators and making representations to the Government.

It is standard practice for the Government to publish a White Paper prior to the publication of draft legislation. This document sets out the Government's settled view of the objectives of the legislation and how it will work. Having published their proposals in this way, governments rarely change their minds about the main content of the legislation. However, they sometimes publish a Green Paper prior to the White Paper, and in this case the proposals are for discussion and may include a range of policy options for consideration. A government may also publish consultation papers on specific aspects of proposed legislation, although this tends to cover the technical implementation of the proposals rather than the principles involved.

Reviewing the pension system: Formal structures

There is no formal structure in the United Kingdom for the review of social security pensions other than the Government itself. Within the Government the responsibility for pensions policy lies with the Department of Social Security, which has as its political head the Secretary of State for Social Services. Also at the political level, there is normally a junior minister within the Department (with the title of Minister of State or Parliamentary Under-Secretary) who has specific responsibility for pensions. Then at the official level there will be a group of career civil servants with responsibility for pension policy, the number depending upon how much work needs to be undertaken.

Apart from the Department of Social Security, three other official bodies have the potential to play a role in the process of pension reform:

- the Social Security Advisory Committee;
- the Government Actuary; and
- the Social Security Committee of the House of Commons.

These are discussed in turn.

The Social Security Advisory Committee

The Social Security Advisory Committee (SSAC) is established under an Act of Parliament to advise the Secretary of State for Social Services on social security matters. It is appointed by the Secretary of State and consists of a chairperson and between ten and 13 members. One member is appointed following consultation with employers' organizations (the Confederation of British Industry – CBI), one following consultation with workers' organizations (the Trades Union Congress – TUC), and one is from Northern Ireland. The Secretary of State is also required to appoint a member who is either chronically sick or disabled or who has experience of the chronically sick or disabled. By custom, the Committee also has members from Wales and Scotland and an ethnic minorities member. Of the other members, most are academics, lawyers or ex-officials with an interest in social security issues.

The SSAC's responsibilities are:

- a general duty to advise the Secretary of State for Social Security on virtually all social security matters except those which are the responsibility of other advisory bodies (e.g. industrial injuries benefits) or have statutory independence (i.e. adjudication systems); and
- to consider and report on social security regulations referred by the Secretary of State.

The SSAC's general advisory role forms the basis of most of its activity, particularly where it decides to pursue issues on its own initiative. Since it was set up, the Committee has examined a wide range of policy issues and published its views on these general topics in its periodic stewardship reports. Wherever possible, the Department involves the SSAC in major social security policy developments, although major changes are sometimes made without prior consultation with the Committee. The SSAC is usually invited by the Department to participate in any public exercise within its territory, for example, the question of state pension age. Although the SSAC has no statutory responsibility for operational matters, it is encouraged to look at the operational implications of changes and service to the public provided by the Benefits Agency.

Most social security regulations also come before the SSAC, the only significant exceptions being regulations which go to other advisory bodies or set benefit rates and contribution levels. When the SSAC has considered the proposed regulations its report has to be presented to Parliament when the regulations are laid down with a statement from the Secretary of State showing what he or she has done (or intends to do) about the SSAC's recommendations. Where the Secretary of State decides that the regulations are needed urgently without a reference to the SSAC before they come into force, the regulations are referred to the Committee after their adoption and a report is then produced. Where the matter becomes urgent after referral to the SSAC, the Secretary of State may proceed to make regulations urgently without waiting for the Committee's report. The report and the Secretary of State's response would then be produced and published at a later date.

The SSAC might have the potential to be an important element in the review of pensions policy. In practice, however, it is primarily reactive rather than pro-active in terms of policy development, and there are few if any significant changes to pension provision that can be said to have resulted from the Committee's work.

The Government Actuary

The Government Actuary and Department, known as the Government Actuary's Department (GAD), are responsible for advising the Government on a range of actuarial matters. The relevance in this context is that the Government Actuary has a statutory responsibility to keep the finances of the National Insurance Scheme under review. In particular he or she produces an annual report on the finances of the National Insurance fund and, more importantly, every five years a long-term review of the National Insurance Scheme's finances, including projections of benefits, contributions and cost. The Government Actuary is also required to produce financial projections of the impact of any legislative changes that are proposed by the Government. All these reports have to be laid before Parliament and thereby become public documents.

The Government Actuary and Department are an independent establishment within the government structure. The Department has over 40 professional staff, of whom around six are employed in the area of social security and pensions. Some of their time, however, is spent in providing advice to foreign govern-ments. The Government Actuary, although a public official, holds professional independence which has been well established by recent incumbents. In particular, where advice has been based on any instructions from the Govern-ment, for example on assumed future rates of unemployment, the Government Actuary's reports always make clear that this is the case and usually provide figures that enable the results to be calculated on other bases. It is important to note, however, that the reports are only a review of the Scheme as it is or as it would be following the changes proposed by the Government, with no scope for suggestions about what, if any, changes are required.

The Social Security Committee of the House of Commons

The third formal mechanism which can review the development of state pensions is the House of Commons' Select Committee on Social Security. This a committee of members of the House of Commons (MPs), with membership drawn from all parties in proportion to their overall parliamentary representation. It is made up of "backbench" members, that is, it does not include government ministers or their opposition shadow ministers, and there is a convention that the chair of this particular Select Committee is held by a member of an opposition party. The Committee has a wide remit covering all forms of social protection and has the power to summon witnesses and documents to aid its deliberations. Within that overall responsibility, the Committee decides for itself what specific subjects it wishes to consider. Thus, for example, it held hearings into the Maxwell scandal in 1992 and also reviewed the recommendations of the Pension Law Review Committee after they were published in 1993. These studies were both about private pension arrangements, but more recently the Committee undertook a study on the general topic of pension provision, producing a report early in 1997 just before the last election.

The Committee's reports tend, in practice, to be written by the chairperson of the Committee, together with relatively limited staff support. There is scope for the Committee to appoint specialist advisers who can help it in its work, but they have no formal position or vote in its deliberations. The aim is usually to obtain an all-party consensus on its recommendations, but there is no obligation on the Government to have regard to their reports. The impact of the Committee on the development of policy largely depends on the individual politicians concerned and, in particular, the chairperson. During the previous Parliament, the chairperson – Frank Field MP – achieved a high profile for the Committee's work, but in practice relatively few of its recommendations have been adopted as government policy and ultimately included in legislation.

Reviewing the pension system: The practice

Although there are formal structures for the review of pensions policy, as described in the previous section, much of the process is actually undertaken on an ad hoc basis. In other words, governments consider the issue when and how they consider it appropriate. Thus, when a Government has formed a view, whether for political or practical reasons, that changes are needed to the system of pensions provision, it will either decide for itself what changes are required or appoint a group of experts to advise on possible modifications. In the latter case it will not be bound by the group's conclusions, although they will inevitably carry some weight.

As an example of how this works in practice, the present Government, as part of its current review of pensions provision, has appointed a group of experts under the title the "Pension Provision Group". Its terms of reference were "to determine the current levels of pensions provision in the UK, and likely future trends; and to report ...", and it is important to note that this does not include specific policy proposals. With representatives from financial institutions and academics, as well as the social partners, its job was to try to establish some sort of consensus on current standards of pensions provision and prospects for the future. However, its membership, terms of reference, timetable and the form in which its finding have been disseminated were all decided unilaterally by the Government. Now that the Group has presented its report, it is entirely up to the Government how far it will accept the guidance that has been offered.

The initiation, scope and timetable of any review of pensions provision in the United Kingdom are, therefore, almost entirely in the hands of the government of the day and its officials. The normal pattern by which reform takes place is that a government is elected with a political commitment, described in its manifesto, to some form of pensions reform. This was the case, for example, following the general elections of 1959, 1964, 1970, 1974 and 1997, although not all these governments were successful in carrying out their intentions during their subsequent term of office. Less often a government will decide during its term of office, without any prior electoral commitment, that changes are required, as for example in 1983 and 1994.

The objectives of any reform tend, as a result, to be fairly well established and it is the job of the politicians and their officials in the Department of Social Security, in consultation with those in the Treasury and other interested departments, to come up with proposals to implement those objectives. Whether this process involves consultation with outside bodies and, if so, the extent of this consultation and with whom it takes place lies largely in the hands of the Government. Such consultation might be entirely on an informal basis, although recent examples in the area of pensions legislation have been more structured, with publically available consultation papers and/or Green Papers setting out a range of options within the Government's overall political objectives. Ministers and/or their officials will hold meetings with such organizations and groups as and when they determine. The sorts of groups that they consult are described below.

Once the provisions of the proposed reform have been established, with or without a period of consultation, the subsequent decisions on their implementation are again entirely in the hands of the Government. Its proposals will be presented in the form of a White Paper, followed by the publication of the bill. Once the bill has been published, the opportunity for significant changes to the legislation are in practice relatively limited. Although, in theory, changes can be made to the legislation, most governments have used their parliamentary majority to push through their proposals with few if any amendments. For example, there were no significant changes made to the last Government's changes to National Insurance pensions in the Pensions Act 1995, following their publication in the White Paper. This is described in more detail in the following section.

There are a range of actors outside government who will seek to have an input to the Government's policies through the opportunities that are offered for consultation, either formal or informal. First, there is a relatively disparate group of organizations which make up what is often described as "the pensions industry". This includes financial institutions, such as insurance companies and investment advisers who manage private sector pension arrangements; consultants such as actuaries and solicitors who advise on the establishment and management of private schemes; and scheme administrators and managers, mainly through the National Association of Pension Funds (NAPF) and the Pensions Management Institute (PMI). Secondly, there are actors who are outside the pensions industry, primarily employers and trade unions but also a number of loosely allied organizations representing pensioners. The third group consists of academics and several policy-based research organizations that are often described as "think tanks". The impact of these various actors varies widely from time to time and issue to issue, as well as with the Government's political complexion. Thus, the trade unions might be expected to have more influence with the present Labour Government than they had with the previous Conservative Government.

The role of these actors in the process of change is limited to the following:

- taking the initiative in making proposals for change to the Government, particularly when the latter has said that it is considering some changes;
- making comments to any group or committee which the Government has established to advise it on its proposals and, possibly, participating through a representative on that advisory body;
- commenting to the Government on its proposals set out in a Green Paper or other consultation documents, if they have been issued;
- commenting to the Government on its proposals set out in a White Paper and/or a bill; and
- lobbying the Government or opposition parties to propose amendments to the legislation during its passage.

Given the largely ad hoc nature of the legislative process and the extent to which decisions are in the hands of the Government, the degree of openness can vary widely. There are no statutory requirements for the process to be open, but there has been an increasing awareness that because of the technical nature of many of the issues involved, there are significant advantages in obtaining input from those with relevant expertise outside the Government.

Reviewing the pension system: The Pensions Act 1995

The last occasion when significant changes were made to the state pension system was with the passage of the Pensions Act 1995. The Act was introduced primarily as a reaction to the Maxwell scandal, when in 1991 an employer was able to remove substantial sums of money from an occupational pension scheme established for its employees. The main purpose of the Act, therefore, was to introduce a range of measures increasing the supervision of private pension schemes and tighter controls on the way they are run. However, the Act also made some important changes to National Insurance pensions. First, and most significant, it provided for a staged increase in the retirement age of women, over the period 2010–20, from the present age of 60 to 65, so that it equalled that for men. Secondly, there were changes to the way in which SERPS benefits are to be calculated in future. Thirdly, the conditions set for pension schemes used for contracting-out purposes were modified, with the primary aim of simplifying the system of contracting-out.

Much of the Act was based on the recommendations of the Pension Law Review Committee, with Professor Goode as chairperson. This Committee had been established by the Government in 1992, in the wake of the Maxwell scandal, to advise on the changes required to the law governing private pension schemes. In view of these terms of reference, it actually has little to do with state provision and strictly falls outside this report. However, it is interesting to note that the Committee was largely made up of representatives of the pensions industry plus an academic, with no formal representation of the social partners. However, there was one member with links to the labour movement, while others had links to employers. The Committee reported in 1993 when the Government made an initial response to its proposals, followed by the publication of a Pensions White Paper in June 1994 and the bill in December of that year. The bill completed its legislative passage in June 1995.

None of the changes to state pensions in the Act arose directly from the recommendations of the Review Committee, although they did mention the need, as far as possible, to simplify the contracting-out process. Instead the three sets of changes arose very much from the Government's own political agenda aimed at shifting the burden of pension provision from the State to the private sector.

The equalization of the state pension age had been a live issue for many years, but previous governments had avoided taking any action in view of what was regarded as a "no-win" situation politically. It was thought either that the cost of equalizing at age 60 would be too expensive, or that equalizing at age 65 would be very unpopular – and not just with women. The issue had been discussed on a number of previous occasions but only started to receive serious consideration from 1991, when the Government issued its own detailed consultative document. This set out the arguments for and against a number of options for equalization. All the actors listed above took the opportunity to respond to the consultative document, together with a number of individuals.

Government ministers and officials subsequently held meetings with the main representative organizations. There was no consensus in the responses, with employers and the pensions industry generally favouring a phased equalization at age 65 and trade unions, pensioners' organizations and individuals favouring early equalization at age 60.

Following the end of this period of consultation, the Government announced in 1993 that it had decided to opt for equalization at age 65, but with its phased implementation deferred until the period 2010 to 2020. Measures to this end were therefore included in the June 1994 White Paper and the bill which followed. During the passage of the bill, there was a public campaign against this particular measure, supported by the trade unions and women's organizations, but this had little impact and the measure was passed unamended in June 1995.

The changes to the method of calculating of SERPS benefits originated solely from the Government. They were first presented in a consultation paper, published in late 1994, as being of a technical nature required to correct earlier errors in the legislation. In practice they will have a substantial effect on SERPS benefits payable in the future, leading to a significant reduction in the cost of this element of state pensions. This led in the consultation period to a suggestion from trade union organizations that the real reason for the changes was to bring about a further reduction in future SERPS benefits. However, the changes outlined in the consultation document were included in the June 1994 White Paper and, despite some debate during the passage of the bill, no changes were forthcoming before it became an Act. The discussions that did take place on the changes were limited in scope because few people really understood their somewhat obscure impact.

The third area of reform affecting the state pension system was in the contracting-out arrangements. The initiative for change was again from the Government, although in this case it was against the background of earlier representations from the pensions industry, as well as comments from the Review Committee, to the effect that the structure of private pension provision needed to be simplified. The Government's proposals were first announced in another consultation document published in late 1994 and became law following the same timetable as the changes to SERPS benefits described above.

It can be seen that the process of reform that culminated in the Pensions Act 1995 was largely based on ad hoc structures, with the Government very much in control at every stage. There has now been a change of government, with the Labour Party committed in their election manifesto to further pension reforms. The manifesto proposals were very general in scope, however, and one of the Government's earliest actions was to initiate a wide-ranging review of pension provision, both state and private. The intention was to encourage the widest possible participation in working out how to implement the Government's broad objectives.

The process of review has had various main elements. First, a consultation document was made widely available in June 1997, setting out the Government's broad objectives for pension provision and inviting comments on how they might be achieved. This stage of consultation was completed by the end of that year.

Secondly, the Government established the Pension Provision Group, as mentioned above, with the task of establishing a consensus about current standards of pension provision and prospects for the future. Its membership consisted of one representative each from the Trade Union Congress (TUC) and the Confederation of British Industry (CBI), together with a consulting actuary, a pension scheme manager, someone from a life insurance company and two academics with backgrounds in economics and gerontology respectively. The aim of the Group was to provide an informed basis for the wider debate, and its report entitled "We all need pensions – the prospects for pension provision" was published in June 1998. The Group has subsequently been retained, at least in the short term, to comment on the development of the Government's proposals.

The third element of the review was a more focused consultation specifically on what are known as "stakeholder pensions". These are a key element in the Government's strategy for improving pension provision and are intended to extend the benefits of having a good private pension to a much larger proportion of the workforce. The document was issued in November 1997 and comments were required by the end of January 1998.

Following these exercises, the Government received a large amount of material in reply, mainly from the actors identified above. It then published a Green Paper early in 1999 which set out its key proposals, but very much in outline. Some of the proposed changes will affect state pension benefits, and legislation to carry these out will be presented to Parliament in the 1999/2000 parliamentary session at the earliest. Other changes intended to promote private "stakeholder pensions" are being brought before Parliament in the 1998/99 session, but these provisions are essentially enabling powers. The detailed arrangements for stakeholder pensions will be set out in statutory regulations and the Department of Social Security undertook detailed consultations about what these should contain with the usual interested parties over the summer of 1999. The consultation process involved six documents on specialist topics and the formation of a group comprising representatives from the main organizations with an interest in stakeholder pensions. At the time of writing, however, it was still unclear exactly when stakeholder pensions would be launched.

Conclusions

The development of policy on the United Kingdom's social security pension system is almost totally in the hands of the Government of the day, with other actors only being involved when and how the Government itself wishes. While there is a limited number of bodies with a statutory responsibility to monitor the development of pensions policy, they have, in practice, had only limited influence on outcomes. Of somewhat greater importance have been the formal and informal consultation arrangements that are generally established on an ad hoc basis as and when a Government concludes, usually for political reasons, that changes to pensions legislation are required. These consultations are usually open to a wide range of organizations and individuals, but in practice the leading role is taken by the pensions industry, the social partners, "think tanks" and, to a more limited extent, organizations representing pensioners. When the Government has concluded what changes are required, in the light of its political objectives and the representations received, it introduces legislation which implements those conclusions.

The wish to achieve a consensus in pension policy and, in particular, finding the right balance between needs and resources, plays only a limited role in the development of policy in this area. Given a parliamentary majority there has been no need and, on many occasions, no inclination on the part of the Government to achieve any sort of consensus around its proposals. The process is only required to deliver the changes that the Government considers politically desirable. While the possibility of reaching some sort of consensus is invariably stated to be a desirable objective, it is not evident that it is a priority in practice.

This process is illustrated by the experience of pension reform in the 1960s, 1970s and 1980s. The 1966 Labour Government's proposals for reform were based on policies developed within the Labour Party's own policy structure, bitterly opposed by the Conservative opposition and dropped when there was a change of government in 1970. The new Conservative Government then introduced its own proposals, which were strongly contested by the Labour Party and, in turn, dropped in 1974 when the latter regained office. The introduction of new legislation in 1975, somewhat unusually, had the support of both main parties, but this consensus only lasted until 1983 when the Conservative Government elected in 1979 decided to break it. The ensuing legislation in 1985 was strongly contested by the Labour opposition. Throughout this period the trade unions invariably supported the position of the Labour Party, while employers' organizations usually, although not always, backed the Conservatives' proposals.

This pattern continued into the 1990s. The Conservative Government's 1995 legislation on social security pensions was generally opposed by Labour and the trade unions. Whether or not it will also be followed during the latest series of reforms being considered by the present Labour Government is still an open issue, however. Everyone agrees on the need for a level of consensus but in practice this has proved difficult to achieve, at least on the central issues of any reform. However, the Pension Provision Group has attempted to provide a common factual basis for the discussions that are taking place, and the figures provided by the Government Actuary about the current and future levels of social security expenditure are invariably accepted by all parties. It has also become clear from the discussions held that there is a considerable amount of common ground on some of the major issues.

Against this background, the strengths of the British system are that:

- it gives expression to the political will of whatever party has achieved an electoral majority, usually as presented in its election manifesto;
- it can sometimes, but not always, provide some clear objectives for the proposed reform;
- given those objectives, the consultations undertaken usually provide the opportunity to interested parties to put their views to the Government on matters of implementation; and
- in more practical terms, the Government Actuary's projected figures for the future cost of state pensions are widely accepted by the parties to the debate.

There are also weaknesses in this approach, however, the most significant being:

- there has been little opportunity or incentive to develop a lasting consensus on the major issues of pension reform;
- the system tends to institutionalize a confrontational approach to the development of policy where, in particular, the social partners almost always adopt conflicting objectives for any reform; and
- the system is not very transparent or necessarily democratic, i.e. it is unclear who is and who is not being successful in putting over their views to the Government.

The public pension system of the United States   3

*Lawrence H. Thompson**

Outline of the public pension programme

Virtually the entire working population of the United States is covered by a single pension programme operated directly by the Federal Government. It is the only universal pension programme in the country, and provides a large minority of the aged with their only source of retirement income.

Administrative responsibilities

Public pensions in the United States are provided almost exclusively through the Old-Age, Survivor and Disability Insurance (OASDI) programme which is operated directly by agencies of the Federal Government. Contributions are collected by the Internal Revenue Service as a fully integrated part of its procedures to collect the federal personal income tax, and benefit payments are made by the Treasury Department. Most of the other functions of the pension programme are the responsibility of the Social Security Administration, an independent agency whose head reports directly to the President. (These other responsibilities include assigning pension account numbers, maintaining earnings information, establishing entitlement to and calculating the amount of benefits, tracking the status of beneficiaries and so on.)

Coverage

The retirement and survivors' portion of the OASDI programme was enacted in 1935 as part of a comprehensive package of income assistance reforms (the Social Security Act of 1935) that also created new programmes of social

* Senior Fellow, The Urban Institute, Washington, DC.

assistance and unemployment insurance. Disability benefits were added in the 1950s. The OASDI programme initially covered only workers in private sector industry and commerce, some 60 per cent of the labour force at that time. Since then, coverage has been extended to the point that some 96 per cent of employees now participate in the programme. During the 1950s, coverage was extended on a mandatory basis to farmers, the self-employed, the armed forces and household workers, and on an optional basis to state and local governments. Railway workers and federal government civilian employees were brought under the programme in the 1970s and 1980s respectively.[1] The only group of any size not participating in OASDI are several million employees of state and local governments (roughly one-third of the total in these sectors) whose employers did not elect to join the OASDI programme and who are covered by alternative pensions. Proposals to bring this last group under OASDI are now being debated seriously.

Benefits

The OASDI benefit structure is a compromise between the flat-rate benefit models and earnings-related models found in various European countries. Although benefits are related to previous earnings, the benefits provided to lower earners represent a larger proportion of their pre-retirement earnings than those provided to higher earners. The normal retirement benefit paid to a worker who had earnings each year equal to the national average wage would amount to 42 per cent of earnings in the year just prior to retirement. In comparison, a worker with 45 per cent of average earnings during working life would receive some 56 per cent of previous earnings, and a worker with 160 per cent, only about 35 per cent.[2]

The normal retirement age is 65, but is slated to increase gradually to 67 between 2000 and 2022. Benefits are available as early as age 62, but if taken before the normal retirement age they are permanently reduced by an amount calculated to produce the total lifetime payment. Currently, benefits taken at age 62 are reduced by 20 per cent relative to those available at age 65. Benefits will continue to be available at age 62 when the normal retirement age rises to 67, but the permanent reduction at that time will be 30 per cent of the normal benefit.[3] Benefits are based on the average of the worker's highest 35 years of wage-indexed earnings and are adjusted for price changes occurring after retirement. Provisions for men and women are identical, and there are no special provisions granting early access to benefits to those who have experienced prolonged unemployment, to workers in particular industries, or to those with extensive years of credits.

Financing

The public pension programme is financed virtually entirely from contributions totalling 12.4 per cent of earnings, divided equally between employer and employee. The self-employed must pay at the combined employer and employee rate. The current contribution rate is higher than needed to finance current benefits, but is projected to become inadequate for this purpose early in the twenty-first century, when the demographic environment will begin to deteriorate. After 2013, current receipts are projected to be no longer sufficient to cover expected benefit payments and administrative expenditure, although it appears that for 20 years the gap between current receipts and current benefits can be covered from interest earnings and by drawing down the accumulated reserves of the OASDI system. Projections suggest, however, that the accumulated reserves will be exhausted by 2032, and, unless there is a change in the law, the system will no longer be able to pay full benefits.

The general budget has never been used as a significant source of revenue for the OASDI programme. The only allocations coming from the general budget are modest sums to compensate the programme for the cost of gratuitous earnings credits that have been granted from time to time to special groups of the population, such as the Americans of Japanese ancestry who were unjustly detained during the Second World War.

Legislative process

All the provisions governing the level and structure of both benefits and contributions are established in law, so that any changes in either require the enactment of a new law. The normal legislative process is influenced by a mixture of constitutional provisions, congressional procedural rules and political traditions. Under the Constitution, laws must be passed in identical form by majority vote of each of the two houses of Congress and approved by the President.[4] The legislative process frequently begins with proposals presented by the President to Congress, and the President can attempt to influence the outcome at each step in the process. Congress is not required to wait for a presidential proposal, however, and may ignore the President entirely until it reaches the last step in the process. When legislation has passed both houses of Congress it is presented to the President, who must either agree to or veto the entire package. The President is not entitled to approve one part and reject another.

Under the Constitution, laws affecting taxes or appropriations (which include virtually all changes in the OASDI programme) must originate in the

House of Representatives. The rules of the House of Representatives provide, further, that legislation affecting OASDI must be first considered and recommended by its Committee on Ways and Means. That Committee makes recommendations to the entire House of Representatives by issuing a report that must be submitted in advance of any debate and is released to the public. The report must explain the legislation being proposed and contain projections of its impact on federal receipts and expenditures in each of the next five fiscal years, as well as projections of its long-term impact on the fiscal operations of the OASDI trust funds.[5]

The Senate is an equal partner in the legislative process, since it has the right to alter any proposal coming from the House of Representatives in any way it wants. In the Senate, OASDI matters are considered by the Committee on Finance. As with its House counterpart, this committee is required to issue a public report explaining any proposals that it believes the full Senate should adopt and containing detailed cost and revenue estimates of the effect of such actions. Once proposals have passed each house of Congress, representatives of the two bodies get together in an ad hoc committee to come up with a compromise proposal. This is then submitted in identical form to each of the two houses and, assuming adoption there, sent to the President.

Consequences of inaction

A combination of the financial arrangements already noted and the legal arrangements that Congress has established for the programme introduce an important element to the public pension debates in the United States. Under the law, benefit payments are not dependent on annual congressional action and will continue indefinitely, *so long as they can be financed from current contribution income and the reserves accumulated in previous years.* If the point were reached where the combination of contribution income and prior years' reserves was insufficient to cover benefit payments, however, pension cheques would be delayed (or reduced) until Congress and the President agreed on a new financing plan.

Financial oversight

Two different kinds of institutions share responsibility for overseeing developments in the OASDI programme: the Board of Trustees of the OASDI trust funds; and periodic social security advisory councils and commissions. Each of these continues processes and procedures that were initiated at the time of the original legislation in 1935.

The tradition of regular financial projections and commission reviews

The initial proposals for a comprehensive social security system were developed by a Committee on Economic Security appointed by President Roosevelt in 1934. Its deliberations led to proposals that eventually became the 1935 Social Security Act.

In developing its report, the Committee on Economic Security prepared fairly detailed projections of future revenues and expenditure under the new Old Age Insurance programme that it was recommending. The report discussed the projected financial flows up to 1980, some 45 years in the future. As Congress debated the legislation, it continued this tradition by including long-range projections of revenues and expenditure in its reports. Out of this experience emerged the practice of preparing regular projections of the financial status of the programme and of conducting periodic reviews by ad hoc committees established to represent a range of views and interests.

The trustees' reports

Responsibility for financial oversight of the programme now rests primarily with the Board of Trustees of the various social security trust funds.[6] These trust funds are special accounts maintained in the Treasury into which all contribution income (and other receipts) are deposited and to which all benefit payments and administrative expenses are charged. The balances in each fund are invested in a special issue of government bonds, which pays interest at the average market rate for long-term government debt but which can be redeemed at par at any time.

The OASDI funds have six trustees. Four are the heads of executive agencies in the Government: the secretaries of the Treasury, Labor, and Health and Human Services, and the Commissioner of Social Security. Each of these officials is a presidential appointee. The other two are private citizens appointed to a four-year term by the President with the approval of the Senate. Of these two "public trustees", one must be from the opposition party.

The major responsibility of the Board of Trustees is to supervise the preparation of annual detailed projections of the financial status of both the OASDI programme and the Medicare health insurance programme. Each spring it reports on the fiscal operations of the programmes during the previous year, adopts a set of economic and demographic assumptions to be used in projecting future operations, and prepares forecasts of revenue and expenses for 75 years into the future. It is required to call attention in the report to any significant gap between projected benefits and projected revenues. By law, its report is submitted to Congress and released to the public in April of each year. The actual projections are prepared by the Office of the Actuary of the Social Security Administration.

Several processes and procedures have evolved over the years to help ensure that the trustee's annual projections are as objective as possible. First, every four years or so, usually in association with one of the periodic social security advisory councils, a committee of leading economists and actuaries is formed to review the assumptions and methods underlying the trustees' reports. This committee issues its own report commenting on the reasonableness of the assumptions and methods. Second, the law now requires that each annual report contain a certification from the Chief Actuary of the Social Security Administration (who is a career civil servant) attesting to the reasonableness of the assumptions, in his or her professional opinion. Third, the public trustees are charged with assuring that partisan politics do not influence the assumptions and methods, and of reporting any concerns they might have directly to Congress. Fourth, Congress has created its own staff for preparing budget estimates – the Congressional Budget Office – which will review and comment on the trustees' assumptions in the course of its work. None of these would necessarily guarantee objective and non-partisan projections, however, in the absence of a strong tradition against political manipulation of this kind of projections by United States government agencies.

The annual report from the Board of Trustees has developed sufficient credibility that it has come to provide the sole source for projections of the long-range financial status of the current programme and the assumptions and methods underlying this report have become the sole basis for projecting the financial impact of policy changes. In this way, the annual trustees' report forms the basis for all discussions of the financial status of the OASDI programme and for analysing the impact of any policy changes being proposed.

Policy development

Policy development has traditionally involved the interaction of ad hoc advisory groups and commissions to help form a consensus about the pace and direction of future policy outside the normal political process. This tradition may be breaking down, however.

The role of advisory councils

Advisory councils and special commissions have played an important role in both OASDI financial oversight and policy development over the years. The advisory council approach allows a designated group to take the time and devote the attention necessary for a full review of all aspects of OASDI policy. Ideally, after such a review, the members will be able to form a consensus about the most desirable policy changes. Where the advisory council membership includes people credible with a wide range of political interests, a consensus that emerges from this process gains immediate credibility with the legislature. The process is particularly valuable in the case of highly complex and technical issues such as those involved in the altering public pension programmes.

When the original Social Security Act was being developed, primary attention was given to the sections offering immediate relief from the Great Depression; the initial pension payments were not scheduled to occur until 1942. In 1937, however, the Senate Committee on Finance and the federal agency responsible for all social security programmes appointed a citizen advisory council to review the 1935 law and make recommendations for changes. The pension programme as we know it today emerged from the work of this Committee. The Committee contained six labour leaders, six industrial leaders, and 13 representatives of the general public. Industrial leaders included the Chairman of US Steel and the President of General Electric. Public members included several of the most prominent economists of the day. Since 1937, virtually every major change to the programme has been enacted only after being considered and recommended by some form of broadly based, officially sanctioned advisory group or commission. Each of these groups was a single-purpose body which ceased to exist as soon as its final report was issued.

Statutory advisory councils

At first, the advisory bodies were appointed on an ad hoc basis, frequently by one of the committees of Congress responsible for OASDI legislation. By the 1960s, a procedure had been created that made a periodic review by an advisory council a regular feature of the OASDI programme. That provision continued in effect until 1995, when it was replaced by a new, and as yet untested, approach.

Under the approach in effect for some 30 years until 1995, the Secretary of Health and Human Services (the official in charge of the executive department in which the Social Security Administration was then located) was required to appoint a new advisory council once every four years.[7] The council was to review all aspects of the programme, including its financial situation, and report its findings and conclusions to the Secretary who was, in turn, required to publish the report and transmit it to Congress. The review was to be completed by the end of the year following the year in which the council was appointed (though councils did not always finish on time).

The law required these advisory councils to consist of 13 persons, contain equal representation of employers' and employees' organizations, and have at least one representative of the self-employed. By tradition, the councils included three or four people representing organized labour and three or four representing employers' organizations. The rest of the members tended to be academics and individuals with a reputation in the field of social affairs and public pension policies.

Traditionally, those picked to represent either employees or employers had to be nominated by a major national trade union or industry association. Employee representatives were usually selected by the leadership of the national trade union federation, the American Federation of Labor and Congress of Industrial Organizations (AFL-CIO).[8] Finding people to represent employers was rather more difficult because there is no parallel national employers' organization in the United States, and for many years most major employers' organizations did not devote much attention to OASDI policy. Nominations would be solicited from a wide range of employers' organizations and industry associations, and three candidates would be selected from the names submitted. Frequently, at least one of these came from the life insurance industry, one of the few industries that did follow OASDI policy carefully. Usually at least one of the individuals selected for other reasons was either a physician or a practising lawyer, which satisfied the need to represent the self-employed.

The selection process was not immune from political involvement. Advisory councils appointed under Republican administrations looked somewhat different from those appointed under Democratic administrations. The degree of political involvement was limited, however, by the knowledge that the results of the advisory council's deliberation would have little impact if the membership was perceived as too slanted in one ideological direction or another.

Breakdown of the advisory council process

The advisory council process worked best in the era when an expanding economy and a favourable demographic situation allowed for programme expansion. Successive councils could develop compromise proposals which maintained a pace of expansion acceptable to both workers' and employers' interests, and which reflected a consensus view of the particular areas for improvement that deserved the highest priority. The process did not prove as effective in dealing with retrenchments when the economic and demographic environment deteriorated.

In 1977 and 1983, two major retrenchments were enacted in the OASDI programme. The first involved fixing a technical error in the way benefits were calculated which, if left unchecked, would have caused benefits to rise over time more rapidly than earnings. The second involved both immediate and delayed benefit reductions designed to deal with both an immediate financing shortfall and the longer-term ageing of the population. In both cases, the consensus that allowed legislation to be enacted emerged outside this traditional advisory council process.

In the case of the 1977 change, technical and policy experts with strong ties to both trade unions and the Republican congressional leadership were able to reach an informal consensus about the exact change that ought to be enacted and convince Congress to make the change. Although the change was also recommended by one of the periodic advisory councils, the informal linkages were the key to creating the political climate in which benefit reductions could occur.

The situation in 1983 was more difficult. Particularly ill-advised benefit reductions had been proposed by the Reagan administration in May 1981, leading to political paralysis in the face of deteriorating trust fund balances. Later that year, Congress and the President agreed to create an ad hoc commission to be composed not only of representatives of workers, management and the public, but of members of Congress representing each house. There were eight Republicans and seven Democrats. The President appointed five members, and the Senate and the House of Representatives each selected five members. The commission began work in February 1982 and achieved virtually nothing for the next ten months. The lack of progress toward consensus can largely be attributed to political posturing associated with the 1982 Congressional elections. In January 1983, the group was finally able to make a compromise proposal for addressing the immediate fiscal problem and present two proposals for dealing with the longer-term fiscal imbalance. At the time the agreement was announced, projections suggested that without congressional action full benefits could continue for only another five months. Once the leaders of both parties and the representatives of the President had agreed on the package, it was quickly enacted by Congress.

The law requiring the regular appointment of advisory councils was repealed when the Social Security Administration was moved out of the Health and Human Services Department and made an independent agency. One feature of that reorganization was the creation of a permanent advisory board consisting of members appointed by the President, and by minority and majority leaders in both houses of Congress. The creation of this new body made the old, periodic advisory councils redundant, and the law mandating their creation was repealed. The last advisory council to meet under the old law was the council that reported early in 1996. Unable to form a consensus about how OASDI should be adjusted to the ageing of the population, it split into three camps, largely on ideological lines.

It is too early to know whether the new advisory board will provide an effective mechanism for developing consensus around needed policy changes, but the early signs are not encouraging. A one-time council tends to have a group dynamic that encourages compromise in order to produce a coherent final report at the end of its deliberations. A member of a continuing advisory body may feel more obliged to be the ongoing representative of a particular group or interest, and may therefore be less willing to compromise that group's interests.

The reform process

As noted earlier, current projections suggest that additional adjustments to either benefits or contributions will be needed to pay full benefits after 2031. These projections have led to much discussion about pension reform and a general consensus about the desirability of enacting such reform as soon as possible. Reform may not occur any time soon, however, owing to the existence of three major barriers.

One barrier to reform is the lack of consensus about the elements of a reform package, as illustrated by the experience of the 1994–96 Advisory Council. In particular, opinion is sharply divided about the advisability of including in the reform the creation of some form of individual, funded accounts. Among supporters of such individual accounts, opinion is divided about the role that the government should play in managing such accounts and whether they should supplement the current package of social security benefits or replace a part of it. Views also differ sharply about the advisability of increasing the retirement age.[9]

A second barrier is that, strictly speaking, current projections suggest that action is not necessary for at least a quarter of a century. Although all profess to agree that early action to resolve the projected financial problems is desirable, many would prefer no action to a reform in a direction that they deem unacceptable. The legislative process in the United States is structured to allow a substantial minority to block any change that they find unacceptable. As long as currently legislated social security benefits can continue to be financed by currently legislated contributions, the lack of a consensus about how the programme ought to be reformed means, most likely, that no change will be made.

Finally, the institutions that were used in the past to help form a consensus about social security changes no longer exist. Although the political dialogue continues, it is not clear how this dialogue will produce the kind of serious bargaining over each of the many policy and legislative details which must be agreed to before a reform package can be adopted. The President sponsored several "town meetings" around the country during 1998 and announced that a White House conference would occur that year. In the past, White House conferences have proved to be excellent vehicles for focusing attention on social problems. They have not, however, proved to be effective mechanisms for reaching a consensus about painful adjustments in major public programmes. Presumably, another ad hoc commission or committee will have to be created to bring the two branches of government and the two political parties together before a compromise can emerge.

Strengths and weaknesses of the American approach

One major strength in the United States is the tradition of regular projections of the financial status of both the OASDI and health insurance programmes and the widespread acceptance of the results of the official projections as an objective assessment of the current fiscal status of the programmes. These projections provide a common set of estimates of the current financial conditions, a common framework for evaluating the fiscal situation and a common set of assumptions and methods for use in analysing the financial implications of alternatives. The widespread acceptance of the trustees' report baseline provides all participants in the debate with the same point of departure and allows the debate to focus directly on the policy choices available, and their impact on future benefits and contribution rates.

A second strength is the requirement that full benefit payments cannot continue in the absence of adequate contribution income. Together with the tradition that general budget revenues are not to be used to finance OASDI benefits, this means that, eventually, an agreement will have to be reached about how benefits and contributions are to be brought into alignment.

American institutions and traditions introduce several serious weaknesses in the pension reform debate, however. First, as a general rule the social partners are less effectively organized in the United States than in many other countries of the Organisation for Economic Co-operation and Development (OECD), and their organizations are even less influential today than they were earlier this century. This institutional weakness complicates the task of forming a consensus about how unpleasant adjustments might be structured. No institution is powerful enough to negotiate a compromise and convince broad elements of society that the particular agreement reached represents the best approach possible.

Second, the current dialogue focuses only on one or another particular aspect of the ageing problem. One set of discussions concerns the OASDI programme, another focuses on private sector pension programmes, and yet another involves public and private sector health insurance programmes for the aged. Little attention is paid to the relationships among these programmes even though all are affected by the same demographic developments. The absence of a coordinated approach is due in part to the fact that responsibility for these various systems is divided among various different government agencies and congressional committees. If there is to be a comprehensive approach to the challenge of the ageing population, some institution or group will have to be created with the authority to look across programmes and balance the interests of all of the important social interests.

A third challenge is the breakdown in the consensus about the relative roles of the public and private sectors in the retirement income system. For 60 years, public policy was based on the assumption that a public, defined benefit pension programme would provide basic coverage, supplemented by voluntary, private arrangements. Now, many argue that the public programme should be replaced in whole or in part by privately managed, individual-based pensions. This new element in the debate has introduced a philosophical gulf that will be difficult to bridge in the near future and, therefore, greatly complicates the process of reaching a compromise consensus reform package.

Summary and conclusions

The public pension programme in the United States was constructed in the late 1930s. Its basic structure has remained unchanged since then. Current projections suggest that the contribution rate now scheduled is sufficient to finance benefits until about 2031. Thereafter, the impact of the ageing of the population will force some combination of benefit cuts or contribution rate increases.

The United States has a strong tradition of preparing and issuing regular long-range projections of the fiscal condition of the public pension programme. There is an equally strong tradition that the programme be financed essentially from employer and employee contributions. The combination of the projected financing difficulties and the tradition against budget finance is creating tension between those who reject all forms of tax increases and those who resist any benefit cuts. At the moment, sharp philosophical differences divide the two groups.

Eventually, some form of ad hoc committee or commission will have to be created to forge a consensus. This is unlikely to happen soon unless the combination of the public debate and the recent difficulties in financial markets causes the philosophical differences to narrow substantially.

Notes

[1] Both groups had been excluded from coverage in the 1930s on the assumption that OASDI coverage was not needed since they already had their own pension programmes. It subsequently became clear, however, that operating separate programmes for these sectors created serious coordination problems. In the 1970s the railway pension system was reorganized and so completely integrated with OASDI that, in effect, railway workers were brought under the universal programme. Since the 1980s, all newly hired civilian employees of the Federal Government have been covered by OASDI.

[2] In 1996, the average benefit awarded to newly retiring male workers was 95 per cent of the theoretical amount calculated for a full-career worker on average earnings. The average benefit awarded a newly retiring female worker was some 60 per cent of this theoretical benefit.

[3] The 30 per cent reduction in benefits taken at age 62 is a smaller reduction than would be necessary to produce the same lifetime benefit stream when the retirement age reached age 67. This departure from past practice on the part of the OASDI was to keep age 62 benefits from falling too low.

[4] Technically, the law must pass both houses of Congress and be presented to the President, who has ten days in which to exercise a veto. A presidential veto can be overridden by a two-thirds vote of each house of Congress. In practice, however, it is highly unlikely that a major change in the OASDI programme which had been vetoed by a President could gain the two-thirds vote needed to override the veto.

[5] Frequently, legislation changing social security is brought to the full House of Representatives under what is called a "closed rule", meaning that general floor amendments are not in order. In effect, the legislation adopted by the Ways and Means Committee must be adopted or rejected by the full House without change. Floor action in the Senate is never restricted in such a way.

[6] There are four such funds, two for the Medicare programme financing health care for the aged, one for the Old Age and Survivors Insurance programme and the fourth for the cash benefits paid under the Disability Insurance programme. These latter two are often treated as if they were one programme with one trust fund.

[7] Since the councils were created in accordance with a statutory mandate, they were often known as "statutory advisory councils".

[8] At times, when one or more large unions were not affiliated with the AFL-CIO, the national federation might be given two seats and the unaffiliated unions allowed to agree on one additional candidate.

[9] A charitable foundation has been sponsoring a series of "town meetings" to discuss social security reform options. Among their preliminary observations is that among those citizens who have had an opportunity to weigh the implications of the various options carefully, support for an increase in the retirement age is much weaker, and for an increase in contribution rates much stronger, than the support for each position among current political leaders. No serious reform is likely until the views of the political leaders and those of the informed population correspond more closely.

Selected bibliography

1998 Annual Report of the Board of Trustees of the Federal Old-Age and Survivors Insurance and Disability Insurance Trust Funds, House Document 105–243, 105th Congress, 2nd Session, 30 Apr. 1998.

National Conference on Social Welfare: *The Report of the Committee on Economic Security of 1935 and other basic documents relating to the development of the Social Security Act: 50th Anniversary edition* (Washington, DC, 1985).

Report of the National Commission on Social Security Reform, Jan. 1983.

US Department of Health and Human Services: *Report of the 1994–96 Advisory Council on Social Security,* 1996.

US Social Security Administration: *Social Security Bulletin, Annual Statistical Supplement, 1997* (Washington, DC, US Government Printing Office, 1997).

Monitoring and reform of pensions in Germany 4

Heinz-Dietrich Steinmeyer*

The German statutory pension system (the state system)

German statutory pension insurance is a contributory system which is basically linked to the exercise of a gainful occupation. As a result, all those in receipt of a salary – workers and employees, other than civil servants – are covered by compulsory insurance. Disabled people working in protected workshops are also covered, as well as certain self-employed groups, such as performing artists, freelance writers and craftworkers, who are subject to economic and social risks similar to salaried workers. The self-employed may also join a statutory pension insurance scheme at their request. Categories of persons not covered may generally join a voluntary scheme.

The German pension system provides benefits based on age (the statutory retirement age is 65, but in practice people usually retire between 60 and 63), reduction in ability to earn and in case of death (widows', widowers' and orphans' pensions). Benefits are calculated on the basis of the average working life for which contributions are payable and amount to about 70 per cent of the previous income for a period of membership of 45 years. Most of the time, it should be said, this period is not completed.

The system is financed from contributions which are currently 20.3 per cent (half each paid by the employer and the employee), and a federal subsidy from taxation which finances 20 per cent of pension-related expenses. The system is financed on a pay-as-you-go basis.

The German statutory pension system and German social security in general are self-administered (*Selbstverwaltung*). This means that the statutory pension insurance institutions – the Federal Insurance Institution for Employees

---

* Professor, Wilhelms-Universität Münster, Westphalia, Germany.

(*Bundesversicherungsanstalt für Angestellte*), the insurance institutions of the Länder (*Landesversicherungsanstalt*) for workers and the Federal Miners' Pension Fund (*Bundesknappschaft*) – are legal entities with their own management bodies. The most important management body is the assembly of representatives, with equal numbers drawn from the insured and the employer. The assembly has the right to make the rules and thereby influence the benefit structure. It also elects the board of directors and the management of the insurance institution concerned, and therefore exercises an influence over day-to-day operation. It does not have any further role in the political or legislative process. With regard to the subject of this study, however, it should be noted that participation by the social partners is central to the system. The employers' representatives are nominated by the employers' organizations, while the representatives of the insured persons are selected in company elections at the same time as trade union representatives.

The legal basis and legislative process

The right to a statutory pension is provided for in the Civil Code, Book 6. Legislation on pensions is essentially passed according to the normal legislative process, with the participation of the *Bundestag* (Federal Parliament) and the *Bundesrat* (Federal Senate), the representative assembly of the Länder. The formal legislative process begins with the deposition of a bill by the Federal Government, by the *Bundestag*, or by the *Bundesrat*. In the latter case, the Federal Government must communicate its draft legislation to the *Bundesrat* beforehand.

In practice, Federal Government bills or bills submitted by parliamentary groups which support the Federal Government are drafted in the ministries. Ministers' preliminary draft legislation, so-called rapporteurs' drafts, are then often communicated to the institutions concerned, before the official legislative process begins, to allow a position to be taken, usually in writing. In fact, the actors concerned are the social partners, in particular, trade unions and employers' organizations, and also, depending on the subject, other bodies such as the association of private insurance companies, the working group on company pension schemes, associations of the insured in the social security system, and so on. Depending on the soundings taken, the bill may, subject to overall policy, be amended. On the other hand, it can be seen clearly at this stage where the opposition of these institutions will come from during the legislative process or how they will try to ensure that their views prevail. The informal means of pressure just described are not based in law but have emerged spontaneously in current practice.

Institutional pressures

On the other hand, the law provides for the Institution of the Social Advisory Council (*Sozialbeirat*). This institution was created decades ago under the 1957 pension reform, which allowed pensions to guarantee the former standard of living and introduced the pay-as-you-go system.

The Social Advisory Council is composed of 12 members, four representatives of the insured, four employers' representatives, a representative of the German Federal Bank (*Bundesbank*) and three representatives of the economic and social sciences. The members of the Social Advisory Council are appointed by the Federal Government for a term of four years. In the case of the representatives of the insured and the employers, the right to nominate belongs in principle to the management of the statutory pension scheme. In fact, the Federation of German Pension Insurance Institutions, the umbrella organization of the statutory pension insurance institutions, plays a key role. The executive board of the Federation nominates, on its own account, a representative of the insured and an employers' representative. It also nominates two representatives, one for the insured and one for the employers, for the workers' pension fund. The central insurance fund for employees, the Federal Insurance Institution for Employees, nominates a representative for the employers and the insured respectively, and the Federal Miners' Pension Fund does the same. The Federal Government may appoint only those nominated, but it has the right to refuse to appoint a person nominated, provided that it gives reasons for so doing. Prior to the nomination of representatives of the economic and social sciences, the Conference of University Rectors must be consulted. The Social Advisory Council also includes a member of the German *Bundesbank* on the basis that his or her views are (also) based on short, medium and long-term financial trends.

The balance of representation of the social partners in this body is assured by virtue of the fact that proposals emanate from institutions which are themselves constituted on the same basis of equal representation.

In practice, people invited to sit on the Social Advisory Council have always up to now been those nominated by the Federation of German Pension Institutions, the Federal Insurance Institution for Employees and the Federal Miners' Pension Fund. The fact that the Federal Government is not legally bound to act on the nomination has only a theoretical significance, the purpose being to provide a check in exceptional cases. The Federal Government would impede the function of this body if, apart from exceptional cases, it sought to influence its composition, in that it consists of representatives of employers and the insured. The Federal Government's role in appointing the representatives of the economic and social sciences is quite different. In this case, the consultation with the Conference of University Rectors is, in practice, a mere formality, so that the Federal Government may, in this respect, determine the composition of the Social Advisory Council as it chooses.

The chair is traditionally held by one of the academic members. Thus, apart from a brief interlude, the economist Professor Meinhold was the Council's first chairperson. Since 1986, his place has been taken by Professor Schmähl, also an economist. There are always two vice-chairpersons representing the insured and the employers.

Under the provisions of the Civil Code, Book 6, applicable in each case, the Social Advisory Council "is responsible in particular for giving an advisory opinion on the report of the Federal Government's Pensions Report". The advisory opinion of the Social Advisory Council is communicated to the legislative bodies by 31 July each year at the latest. Based on the latest information on the number of insured and pensioners, the Pensions Report contains primarily the revenue and expenses, and the fluctuation reserve, model calculations on trends in revenue and expenses, and the fluctuation reserve and contribution rates necessary in each case for the next 15 calendar years. It also contains an overview of the forecast financial trends for pension insurance over the next five years, based on current medium-term economic forecasts. Thus the Pensions Report and the Social Advisory Council's advisory opinion mainly concern the financial evolution of statutory pension insurance. Bearing in mind the crucial importance of this aspect, the role of these two documents is examined in full.

Until the 1992 Pension Reform Act came into force, the activity of the Social Advisory Council was linked to the Government Pensions Actuarial Report, the scope of which was much more limited. In practice, it dealt with the financial movement of pension insurance over the following 15 calendar years, but in general its brief was much narrower.

The law of 19 December 1997, to finance a complementary federal subsidy, also provides that, from 1997, the Pensions Insurance Report and the Social Advisory Council's opinion should also mention the possible repercussions of raising the retirement age on the labour market, the financial situation of the pension insurance system and other government budgets. Once during each session of the *Bundestag*, the Pensions Report and advisory opinion must be supplemented by information on benefits provided by other pension schemes financed wholly or in part from public funds (for example, the civil service pension scheme) and how they are financed, the situation of pension scheme beneficiaries in terms of revenue, and the aggregate benefits provided by these schemes. The supplementary information (concerning raising the age limit) imposes on the author of the Pensions Report and, by the same token, the Social Advisory Council, the obligation to keep a close watch on the repercussions of any change in the law and, thus, to the statutory pension system. The other additional information mentioned extends the scope of its opinion beyond the field of the statutory pension system to encompass all pension schemes, including private ones.

There is also a hierarchy to these opinions. They are exhaustive with regard to systems financed from public funds, while, in the case of other pension schemes, the only aspects considered are those related to the beneficiaries' incomes or the aggregate benefits from different schemes.

This extension of the scope of the work also reflects the development of the work of the Social Advisory Council which, in the face of the interdependence of the various systems of protection, interpreted its mission in a broader sense than just covering statutory pension provision.

On the policy front, the Social Advisory Council exercises influence through its advisory opinions based on its special expertise and approved by the social partners. Where the various representatives on the Social Advisory Council are unanimous, the Federal Government can scarcely ignore its views. The Social Advisory Council also has an indirect influence on policy by virtue of the fact that senior officials in the Ministry of Labour and Social Affairs always attend its meetings. The Federal Government invites the Social Advisory Council to give its views whenever legislation on pension reform is being considered or is in the process of adoption.

The Social Advisory Council's influence varies depending on the degree of political controversy aroused by pension reform. In the case of the 1992 reform, adopted with a broad parliamentary consensus, the Social Advisory Council's influence in the preparatory stages was considerable since, as we have already seen, its opinion reflects the views of the social partners. It was quite different in the 1999 pension reform (adopted in September 1997), which took place in a general political climate marked by confrontation and which did not spare the Social Advisory Council. The conflict situation is naturally reflected by the fact that the German Federal Government that took up office in 1998 has repealed substantial parts of the 1999 pension reform. In the case of the 1999 Pension Reform Act, the function and the role of ad hoc expert committees set up by the Government and the political parties was more important. That is why we can say that the influence and role of the Social Advisory Council are crucially dependent on a basic consensus. At the same time, in such situations, the role of the Social Advisory Council is precisely to promote the formation of a broad consensus.

The Social Advisory Council's influence on the 1992 and 1999 pension reforms cannot be demonstrated by specific examples of specific components of the reforms. That does not mean that the Council does not have any influence –

quite the contrary. However, it is locked into a network of contacts between the social partners and the Government at other levels. In addition, through the presence of senior officials from the Ministry of Labour and Social Affairs at its meetings, the Social Advisory Council also has an influence on government measures, since its assembled expertise, and the views of the social partners represented there, are expressed in the political or legislative process.

The opinion of the Social Advisory Council on the annual Pensions Report is transmitted with that report to the legislative bodies. It is published as a parliamentary document for consideration by the *Bundesrat* and the *Bundestag* and their committees, but it is also available for examination by the general public. The same applies to the Pensions Report that must be submitted once during each parliament. The other opinions are submitted to the Federal Government for internal consultation.

In the case of advisory opinions on proposed reforms, the Federal Government takes the initiative, approaching the Social Advisory Council and inviting its views. The Council has a mission of its own, described in more detail in the law, which it fulfils without any specific initiative because it is part of its legal requirements. On the other hand, the tasks are described in a fairly general way, so that, within this framework, the Council has a certain latitude in structuring its programme. In the area of social policy, that can also lead to a degree of direction.

Where the opinions relate to the financial outlook for the pension insurance system, they are based on figures and calculations by the Federation of German Pension Institutions, the Federal Office of Statistics and the *Bundesbank*. Two of these institutions are represented in the Social Advisory Council. In practice, the calculations as such are not questioned, but accepted as correct given the standing of the institutions concerned. The debates, both in the Social Advisory Council and in public, are more concerned with which of the assumptions on which the calculations are based are the most realistic. The predominant concern is the direction of trends in unemployment or incomes.

The network of contacts with social groups

The work of the Social Advisory Council must be seen in the context of a network of various contacts and forms of cooperation between the social partners and the Government. The network ranges from ad hoc expert committees to round tables organized by the Federal Chancellery (Chancellor's symposiums), during which there are meetings between the presidents of the main trade unions or the German Confederation of Trade Unions (DGB) and presidents of employers' associations or the Confederation of German Employers' Associations (BDA), to the institutionalized joint action of the social partners in the self-administration of social insurance and "employment pacts". In the Social Advisory Council, the social partners are normally represented by directors of associations.

The ad hoc expert committees set up by the Federal Government are often structured in such a way that, alongside academic experts in the subject of the expert committee in question, there are also representatives of the social partners. In general, however, the sphere of influence of these committees is even wider. Depending on the subject under examination, representatives of other interest groups are called in, for example, in the case of women's pension insurance issues, the Council of German Women. The influence of these expert committees in the political process varies enormously from case to case. If, as usually happens, the social partners are represented on the expert committee, this strengthens the committee's political influence. In complex issues, in particular, the influence of the academics is also extremely powerful.

In addition, these expert committees, like other comparable bodies and committees, also include representatives of the churches. In setting principles, their presence can be explained by the desire to base political decisions on the broadest possible social base. It should also be borne in mind that the churches regard it as quite natural to wish to express views on social policy issues and be involved in the relevant decisions.

Following the October 1998 election, an employment pact was concluded, but without the churches. No doubt the Federal Government considered that restricting it to the main actors (government, trade unions and employers) – at least initially – would make it more effective, but this has not so far proved to be the case. Despite several meetings concerning the pact, a kind of stalemate in social policy seems to have developed. Some trade unions have even threatened to leave the pact.

Inclusion of the social partners in decisions on social policy

As a result of all these measures, the social partners, through negotiation and dialogue, are included in the decision-making process in what can only be described as informal ways because of their legal status, but which, in fact, may or should lead directly to effective decisions. One should think in this respect of the Federal Government's negotiations with the social partners on the options for limiting increases in statutory pension contributions during the preparatory stage of the 1999 pension reform. After the end of the negotiations, the participants said that there was agreement on a wish to amend the right to statutory pension benefits and indicated that, from the point of view of preserving legitimate confidence, the date of the negotiations for the transitional arrangements was fixed. An uninformed observer unfamiliar with the German decision-making process would inevitably have had the impression that a definitive and mandatory decision had been taken, although in reality the Federal Government had merely said that it would include a bill in the legislative procedure based on the outcome of those negotiations.

From the German point of view, it may be concluded that amendment of national systems now makes such a procedure essential. The Federal Republic of Germany, by seeking a consensual solution, thus managed to avoid the social conflict unleashed by the French approach in 1995 and 1996, which ultimately led to a settlement similar to that reached in Germany, a social summit. On the other hand, decision-making processes based on consensus may have the disadvantage that perhaps essential radical cuts can be made only with great difficulty.

With the employment pacts, the Federal Government has not achieved a great deal. The central idea is that the social partners agree to participate and undertake to act in accordance with government policy in their sector of activity. The system only works as long as there is a basic consensus and fails when tensions arise, as was ultimately the case with the previous Federal Government.

Conclusions

In general, the method of associating the social partners, other social groups and academics in the process of social policy, in an institutionalized framework, has proved its worth in Germany. It has also certainly helped ensure that proposed reforms in the pension insurance sector have generally been backed up to now by a fairly broad consensus.

Nevertheless, the situation of the employment pact and the 1999 pension reform, which was adopted in a climate of controversy and which the new Federal Government has re-opened in part, shows that this does not always happen and that the coordination described above is no guarantee of consensus solutions.

It also emerged that there is an advantage in limiting the number of members of the Social Advisory Council and the other, informal, groups, since that probably makes it easier to reach a consensus. The comparable body in the broadest sense established under the Health Insurance Act – the Concerted Action on Health – is much more varied in its composition, including representatives of health insurance funds, the Association of Private Health Insurers, doctors, dentists, hospital managers, chemists, pharmaceutical manufacturers, trade unions, employers' associations in the Länder and community associations, and one representative each of health workers, health care providers, health resorts and spas, care workers, independent welfare organizations, associations of disabled persons, and consumers' associations. There are also representatives of various federal ministries. In this body, those involved in health care administration must provide the insured with treatment appropriate to their medical condition and apportion the costs fairly. At the same time, they must make proposals for medical and economic policy and develop projects to increase revenue, efficiency and profitability in health care, and ensure their coordination. Given that in this area there are usually distributional conflicts and the Association is very vast, in practice the outcome is usually rather general declarations and discussions that never produce a clear decision.

The conclusion must be that such a body must be kept to a reasonable size. Moreover, the consensus solution only works well in an area where consensus is easy because of the nature of the subject. However, that does not mean that bodies of this kind are of no value in other areas marked by controversy such as, in Germany, health care. The mere fact that the participants try to agree on a number of specific points, which may then lead to usable results, even if they are mostly general in nature, has the advantage that the participants are formally part of a body involved in the social policy process.

Taken as a whole, the German system of institutional participation seems well suited to making the process of social policy less sensitive to conflict and more results oriented. The institutions which use experts seem particularly well equipped for this task.

The Japanese experience of review and reform of public pension schemes

5

Jean-François Estienne* and Kiyoshi Murakami**

The state pension system and the legislative process

A brief description of the state pension system

1. State schemes[1]

The public pension scheme in Japan has four elements: a universal pension system; a compulsory supplementary pension scheme for private sector employees; mutual pension funds; and pension funds for non wage earners.

1.1 A universal pension system (*kokumin nenkin*)

This is a universal contributory system which covers a population defined on the basis of age. Membership (in theory[2]) is subject to two conditions: residence in Japan and being aged between 20 and 60 years. There are in theory 70 million members. The scheme was originally set up in 1959 for people who did not belong to company pension schemes (see below), and became universal in 1986.

The scheme places the members in three categories, based on marital status and occupation. Category 1 is defined by default and includes those who do not belong to the other two categories. Category 2 consists of wage earners, and category 3, spouses of wage earners.

The contribution for category 1 (neither wage earners nor spouses of wage earners) is a monthly flat-rate of 13,300 yen (at 1 April 1998). In principle, the contribution is compulsory for all three categories, but in the case of category 1, the payment is de facto voluntary. For category 2, the basic contribution is

* Ecole des Hautes Etudes en Sciences Sociales, Paris.

** Former lecturer at the University of Tokyo, former administrator of the Nihon Dantai Life Insurance Co. Ltd, and former member of the ILO Social Security Actuarial Committee.

included in the earnings-related scheme (see below), while for category 3 (wage earners' spouses), the basic contribution is free.

As regards benefit entitlements (at 1 April 1998), the minimum period of membership is 25 years and benefits are payable from age 65 (rising by stages from 60 to 65 for persons in category 2). The full rate is paid for membership of 40 years at age 65 (rising by stages from 60 to 65 for persons in category 2). In this standard case, the monthly benefit is 66,625 yen.

The basic scheme is financed on a pay-as-you-go basis with reserves.[3] The funding comes, in equal parts, from three sources: contributors, employers (through the employees' scheme) and the State. The Ministry of Health and Social Affairs is responsible for supervising and administering the system.

1.2. A compulsory supplementary pension scheme for private sector employees (kôsei nenkin hoken)

This scheme was established by a 1954 Act, to replace a previous scheme established in 1942. Membership of the scheme for persons in category 2 of the basic regime (or, where applicable, a special scheme) is compulsory.

The contribution rate (at 1 April 1998) was 17.35 per cent of the basic monthly salary (excluding bonuses) with a monthly ceiling of 590,000 yen. Bonuses, which generally amount to three or four months' salary, are not subject to this contribution, but since the 1994 reform (see Annex 3) are subject to a special deduction of 1 per cent. Bonuses are not included in the base for calculation of the benefit. Contributions are shared equally between employees and employers.

As for benefits (at 1 April 1998), the minimum period of membership is 25 years, and benefits are paid starting from the sixtieth birthday. In the standard case, at age 60 and after 40 years' contributions, the full monthly pension is 167,625 yen (of which 66,625 yen is the flat-rate pension[4] and the balance is earnings related). The flat-rate element in fact corresponds to the basic pension. The pension due to the compulsory supplementary scheme is the balance, i.e. 101,000 yen.

The compulsory supplementary pension scheme for private sector employees is managed on a pay-as-you-go basis with reserves. It is funded on an equal basis by employers and employees. The Ministry of Health and Social Affairs is responsible for the supervising and administering of the system.

1.3. Four special schemes known as mutual pension funds (nenkin kyôsai kumai)

These schemes operate on the model of the compulsory supplementary pension scheme for private sector emploees, with higher contribution rates (about 20 per cent against 17.35 per cent) and higher benefits (about 135,000 yen compared with 101,000 yen).

These are the special schemes for central government civil servants, local government employees, teachers in the private sector, and the agricultural sector. Each scheme is supervised by the ministry responsible for the sector concerned: the Ministry of Finance for the central government civil service scheme, the Ministry of Internal Affairs for local government employees, the Ministry of Education for the private sector teachers' scheme and the Ministry of Agriculture for the agricultural sector scheme.

1.4. Pension funds for non wage earners

Established in 1991, these funds, membership of which is voluntary, are capitalized and organized around particular professions or regions. In this defined contributions and benefits system, the contributor chooses a contribution level which guarantees him or her a specified amount of annuity.

The Ministry of Health and Social Affairs is responsible for supervising and administering the system. These are the only state schemes funded on a purely capitalized basis.

2. Company schemes[5]

Company schemes entail two elements: pension funds and end-of-service benefits.

2.1. Pension funds (kôsei nenkin kikin)

These funds are an original measure, first introduced in 1966: these defined benefit schemes, operating on the basis of capitalization, are funded in part by a reduction in the compulsory contribution to the compulsory supplementary scheme. Thus the funds have two components, one of substitution to replace the benefits of the compulsory supplementary scheme, to which employees contribute half, and the other a supplementary component, all of it paid by the employer. The existence of the substitution component of the Japanese pension funds distinguishes them from the British "contracting out" system. The supervision by the Ministry of Health and Social Affairs of these funds is designed to ensure the long-term viability of the substitution component. The inclusion of the latter in the fund is a form of delegation by the state scheme. It is more a partial transfer than an exit from the basic scheme.

Participation in the pension fund is compulsory for all employees of companies which are members of the fund.

The contribution rate, which may vary slightly from one fund to another, is typically 3.5 per cent for the substitution component, shared equally between the employee and the employer. For the supplementary component, the rate is usually between 2 and 6 per cent, paid wholly by the employer.

For the benefit relating to the substitution component, the rules for calculation are the same as for the compulsory supplementary scheme, while the rules for awarding and calculating the pension from the supplementary component are specific to each pension fund.

The funds do not directly manage their own assets. There is an obligation to delegate this function to financial institutions such as trustee banks or life insurance companies. These bodies provide depository, reporting, actuarial, benefit payment and asset management functions. The latter may now be exercised by management consultants, some of which have foreign capital and are currently very popular in Japan.

The Ministry of Health and Social Affairs is responsible for supervising these funds. The financial institutions to which they entrust their assets are under the auspices of the Ministry of Finance.

2.2   End-of-service benefits

These arrangements are the oldest form of pension in Japan and are still very widespread. Originally intended to reward employees' loyalty, one of the most common bases for calculating end-of-service benefits is length of service. These benefits are funded entirely by the employer. The benefit is paid when the employee leaves the company, most frequently on reaching retirement age. However, other events resulting in employees' departure are often covered, such as voluntary resignation (generally a reduced benefit), death before retirement age, dismissal by the company (other than for a serious offence, when the benefit may not be paid) or promotion to the status of administrator.

It is not compulsory to have an end-of-service benefit scheme, but it is very common and end-of-service benefit rules are annexed to the company's memorandum and articles. Each company is free to set its own end-of-service benefit scheme rules. Once fixed, they apply to all established employees. As part of the general conditions of employment, such benefits are supervised by the Ministry of Labour, which allows the maximum freedom in the way the benefits are determined. The Ministry of Labour is concerned to satisfy itself on two points: the agreement of employees' representatives and the absence of discrimination.

The accounting and financial provision for end-of-service benefit commitments can be done internally by creating reserves in the employer's balance sheet, or externally by creating a trust, or by a combination of the two methods. The trust is set up in a "trust bank" or a life insurance company. The funding of end-of-service benefits comes under the supervision of the Ministry of Finance.

A brief description of the legislative process

The Constitution of 3 November 1946 made Japan a constitutional empire. The Parliament (Diet) consists of an upper chamber (252 councillors elected for six years) and a lower chamber (500 deputies elected for four years, except in the case of dissolution).

Japanese legislative practice, despite appearances, leaves wide powers to the administration. Bills are drafted by the ministries themselves. Consultations on major reforms are through consultative committees, called *shingikai* (see below).

When the committee has submitted its report (the final version is drafted by civil servants), there are consultations between the ministry and the party in power (mainly the Liberal Democratic Party (LDP),[6] which has dominated politics since the Second World War). The bill is then passed to the Consultative Committee on Pensions, which makes observations that are recorded.

The bill is then discussed in parliamentary committee, before a debate and vote in Parliament. In most cases, the amendments requested in public by members of Parliament are minimal or symbolic. The civil service, in principle answerable to the representatives of the people, has a predominant voice in the reforms. However, the (rare) subjects where it is not possible to reach a political consensus, and on which public opinion is divided, unleash a real parliamentary debate. Such political confrontations may delay, significantly amend or even reject the bill prepared jointly by the civil service and the ruling party or coalition.

Thus, pension reform has, on many occasions, been the scene of long and bitter political struggles, as in 1959. In 1965, the law on the establishment of pension funds met with strong opposition from trade unions and the parties of the left.

In the case of the 1980 reform, the administration, faced with the opposition of many actors, including employees' representatives, in an act of self-censure abandoned the proposal to raise the retirement age. As the Japanese believe, rightly or wrongly, that they are suffering from an ageing population, unless something untoward happens, pension reform no longer seems to arouse political debate, but is regarded by public opinion as a matter for experts. However, as the LDP no longer has a majority in the upper chamber, the debates and negotiations on the 1999 reform could be long and hard.

The status and role of public institutions involved in pension review and reform

Article 81–4 of the 1954 Act which established the compulsory supplementary pension scheme for private sector employees (*kôsai nenkin hoken*) set a maximum period of five years for review of the scheme. The same requirement applies to the basic scheme.

During the setting up of the present system, decisions were taken in a variety of ways, depending on the different degree of involvement and powers of each of the actors: the civil service, national representation, the social partners and the degree of public reaction. In 1942, during the authoritarian period, a capitalized employee's scheme was introduced. From 1946 to 1959, during the period of reconstruction following the Second World War, the basic scheme was created. This period was characterized by intense consultations, debates and political conflict, some of it in public. The social partners were very active, with many, often intense debates in Parliament. The preparatory period to the creation of a comprehensive system concluded in 1973. Although this period ended on a relatively consensual note (1973 was proclaimed Year I of the Social Society), some stages gave rise to lively opposition.

During the period when the system was being established, attempts at adjustment (such as the proposed reform of 1980) began. At this time, two committees – the Consultative Committee on Social Insurance and the Consultative Committee on the Basic Pension – were active. The former represented the social partners; the latter did not, since at the time the basic pension was for people who did not belong to another scheme, particularly a company scheme.

The stage of completion and initial adjustments ended with the 1986 reform. The Consultative Committee on Pensions (*nenkin shingikai*), had just been set up under the Ministry of Health and Social Affairs (the first meeting of the new committee was held on 24 October 1985). Effectively an amalgamation of the two old committees which it replaced (social insurance and basic pensions), the new committee had less representation of the social partners. The Consultative Committee on Pensions was still not part of the proposal process, but the Council on Administrative Reform (*rinchô*) was very much involved. It was created in 1980 by the Agency for Administrative Coordination; its chairperson is not a civil servant, but the President of the Employers' Federation (*keidanren*), and chairperson of Toshiba. The Council's mission was to ensure that escalating public expenditure was kept in check. It played a conservative role in proposed pension reforms. Its influence declined in the course of time and it was not to play a major role in the 1986 reform, which already proposed some changes. This reform established the predominant role of the supervising ministry, more particularly the Pensions Office (*nenkin kyoku*) in the Ministry of Health and Social Affairs. The Director of the Office at the time, Mr Yamaguchi, was regarded as a skilful and effective reformer.

The period of forward planning and proactive management,[7] since 1986, aimed at preserving the future balance of schemes and a degree of equity between the generations (if the latter aspect is not taken into account, there will be cases where the retirement pensions will be higher than the net salary of some active employees). The 1994 reform is an example of this, as is the 1999 reform currently in the proposal and drafting stage. The last two reforms confirm the pre-eminent position of the Pensions Office in the reform process, including management of the proposal stage. The instrument of the proposal is the Pensions Advisory Committee.

Characteristics of the Shingikai, in particular the Pensions Advisory Committee (nenkin shingikai)[8]

The consultative committees can cover a wide range of subjects, once important reforms are envisaged. The Consultative Committee on Pensions is a special case, however, since it sits almost continuously because of the requirement for a five-yearly review. The constitution, organization of work and the composition of the committee are typical of normal government practice in Japan.

The creation of a consultative committee is often the product of a consensus between the administration and the political class on the need for reform. The parties concerned (private sector, social partners for social issues, or other groups depending on the subject) may be consulted.

The aim of the civil servants, who manage the process and draft the final report, is to consult the parties concerned.

The civil service is actually represented in the Committee. In the case of pensions, the State is not only the regulator, but also a player. The civil servants who sit on the Consultative Committee on Pensions thus also have responsibilities in pension bodies.

In the past, *shingikai* were chaired by senior civil servants, but in the face of criticism of the predominant role played by the civil service in these committees, the chairpersons are no longer civil servants from the administration managing the reform.

The academic world is always represented on the consultative committees: university professors lend credibility and expertise on the issues and the methodology. They also play a part in the analysis and critique of proposals. Depending on the personality of each professor, their contribution may be confined to the institutional or academic aspect, or may take the form of suggestions or criticism (see "The rules of the game", below).

Civil society, in this case the contributors, is the third element of the membership of the committees. In the case of pensions, they are the social partners. Lastly, an actuary, close to the ministry, also sits on the Committee. Pensioners, who do not constitute a formal group, and do not have any form of representation, are absent from the Consultative Committee on Pensions.

The composition of the committees demonstrates the desire to balance the three elements. If one of them were to dominate, as happens in some committees, this could introduce a bureaucratic, academic or lobbyist bias, depending on the predominant element.

The rules of the game

In Japan, there is a proverb civil servants use which goes: "Listening to the committee is to harvest the opinion of the people". In fact, civil servants control:

- the establishment of committees;
- the appointment and reappointment of committee members;
- management of the work schedule;
- drawing up the agendas for meetings;
- the secretariat and drafting of minutes;
- the drafting, publication and distribution of reports;
- communication with other authorities: executive, legislative (especially the LDP), and the media; and
- management of the post-report stage.

Functioning of the Consultative Committee on Pensions

The above "rules of the game" should not give rise to the idea that the committee is just a façade. The report that it draws up is not always unanimous, because opinions diverge and these differences may be reflected in the report. Traditionally, employers' representatives plead for moderation of contributions, while trade unions are concerned with benefit levels. The diversity and any unpredictability comes mainly from the academics. This diversity is not without some benefit to the ministry: as the report-writer, it can highlight those opinions and options which suit it. The same applies to the Consultative Committee on Social Security. The representatives of the parties concerned, notably the employers' associations and trade unions' work in conjunction with the political parties with which they are most in sympathy. They have a real influence, even partial, in drafting the final report. The report of the deliberations of the committee is now made public. However, civil servants control the whole process and may have a great influence on the content and the way the consensus is expressed.

Distribution of the review, publication of results and consultation with interested parties

The review, in this case the report of the Consultative Committee on Pensions, is distributed by the Ministry of Health and Social Affairs. The report is first submitted to the responsible minister, and then, almost simultaneously, to the press. (In Japan, government information is issued through press clubs, made up of accredited journalists. Foreign journalists, even those with a perfect command of Japanese, are not allowed to be members of these press clubs. Separate sessions, held later, are organized for foreign journalists). The press thus takes charge of the publication of the results. After an initial account of the information contained in the report, the media publish analyses by experts or politicians.

Consultation with the parties concerned (described in the previous section) is supposed to have taken place during the committee consultation process. However, interested parties who so wish have other opportunities to try and influence the final text: while the bill is being drafted, via the ruling party or parties, or via the party with which they are in sympathy, during the parliamentary process.

The process of pension reform in Japan

The reform process is initiated by the Pensions Office (*nenkin kyoku*) in the Ministry of Health and Social Affairs. It is sometimes said in Japan that the quality of the reform is linked to the personality and talent of the Head of the Pensions Office.

The stages are as follows:

Stage 1: deliberations in the Consultative Committee on Pensions

The Committee meets about twice every three months, for a period of some 18 months (depending on the circumstances, the length and frequency of meetings may vary).

Stage 2: drafting of the report

The Chairperson of the Committee, working with civil servants, appoints three or four members of the Committee as rapporteurs.

Stage 3: submission and publication of the report

The report is submitted to the Minister of Health and Social Affairs, and almost immediately communicated to the press.

Stage 4: first draft of the bill

Based on the report, but very loosely, civil servants draw up the first draft of the bill. During this process, there is consultation between the civil servants in the Ministry of Health and Social Affairs, the Ministry of Finance and the ruling party, in this case the LPD (the latter has a pensions review committee: *jimintô nenkin seido chôsakai*).

Stage 5: opinion of the Committee on the first draft of the bill

The first draft of the bill is submitted to the Consultative Committee on Pensions. The members of the Committee give their views, which are recorded.

Stage 6: opinion of the Committee on Social Security

The first draft of the bill, accompanied by the opinions of the Consultative Committee on Pensions, is submitted to the Consultative Committee on Social Security. The latter also gives its opinions, which are recorded.

Stage 7: submission to the Prime Minister

Before submission to the Prime Minister, some provisions may be revised to take account of views expressed by members of the two committees.

Stage 8: presentation to the Diet

As co-drafter with the Ministry of Health and Social Affairs, the ruling party will seek the adoption of the text as presented. Usually, a series of negotiations leads to the drafting of amendments and their eventual adoption. As the ruling party is close to the employers, the concessions demanded by the opposition in exchange for the adoption of the text concern more generous pension benefits and a limit on contribution increases. With respect to the 1999 reform, the LDP had a majority in the lower chamber but not the upper chamber. There may therefore be debates, and concessions demanded and obtained, due to both the ruling party's weak political position and the fact that the new bill contains reductions in benefits and increases in contributions. The strict ministry timetable (submission of the report to the Minister in October 1998, presentation of the bill to the Diet in early 1999 and adoption of the bill in April 1999) could not be met in the event of serious parlia-mentary debate.

Illustration of national experience in the last pension reform: The main elements considered for reform in 1999[9]

Timetable and content of the 1999 reform

1. Timetable for the stages of the reform

- May 1977: constitution of the committee and start of work; 31 meetings were held, the last on 9 October 1998.
- March 1998: publication of the White Paper on pensions: this was a first in Japan.[10] Published by the Ministry, in its forecast section it contains a set of five scenarios, drawn up by civil servants in the Pensions Office. The publication of the White Paper represents the views of the Office and is separate from the work of the Consultative Committee on Pensions.
- 9 October 1998: submission of the report to the Minister and the press.
- November 1998: drafting of the bill by the civil servants and submission to the Consultative Committee on Pensions, and consultations with the LPD and the Consultative Committee on Social Security.
- December 1998 or January 1999: receipt of comments by members of the Consultative Committee on Pensions and submission of the document to the Consultative Committee on Social Security.
- Around February 1999: presentation of the bill in the Diet and debates. During the legislature, the press comments widely on the content of the bill and reports the debates in the Diet and any amendments to the bill.
- End of April 1999 (ministry target): adoption of the bill.

This deadline is more realistic than the previous one, set for April 1999. The new bill was being prepared for adoption at the end of that year, with a view to entry into force by April 2000.

2. Content of the 1999 reform

2.1 Justification of the reform

The reform is presented as inevitable as a result of the "ageing of the population". This is now attributed not only to people living longer but also to the decline in the birth rate.

There is also, according to the Ministry, a contribution threshold beyond which a rise is no longer acceptable. The Ministry believes this threshold to be 30 per cent.[11]

Taking into account the accounting and demographic projections, the contribution rate for the compulsory supplementary scheme for employees would rise from 17.35 per cent in 1998 to 34.3 per cent in 2025.

2.2 Proposal of five scenarios

The five scenarios were drawn up not by the Committee but by the Pensions Office. According to the civil servants in the Office, the five options are not the reform scenario, but simply a document to fuel public debate. However, some observers and journalists think that the median plan ("C" in the list below) represents the objective of the Pensions Office.

- Scenario A: level of benefits unchanged. The only variable is the contribution rate. This then becomes 34.3 per cent of monthly salary or 26.4 per cent of the annual salary in 2025. According to the ministry, the bonus represents an additional four months' salary.
- Scenario B: monthly contribution: 30 per cent; annual contribution: 23 per cent; benefits: -10 per cent.
- Scenario C: monthly contribution: 26 per cent; annual contribution: 20 per cent; benefits: -20 per cent.
- Scenario D: monthly contribution: 20 per cent; annual contribution: 15 per cent; benefits: -40 per cent.
- Scenario E: this radical scenario advocates the abolition of the compulsory supplementary scheme, with the State confining itself to the basic pension. The question of the "sacrificed generation" is not settled, but it is calculated that compensation for lost entitlements would amount to 10 yen million per contributor.

The earnings replacement rates announced are respectively: scenario A: 62 per cent; B: 55 per cent; C: 50 per cent; D: 37 per cent. It should be noted, however, that these replacement rates are based not on final salary but on a career average salary.

Other provisions, or rather omissions, in the Pensions Office presentation tend to reduce the benefits, notably:

- no mention of pensions between ages 60 and 65 in the models presented;
- no mention of indexation, when the pension legislation provides for index linking of the basic pension to inflation.

The failure to mention the above two points shows the way the Ministry hopes, by its silence, to leave itself room for manoeuvre to announce or apply measures or proposals outside the traditional decision-making process. The fact of not mentioning, for example, pensions between ages 60 and 65 should not be interpreted as a unilateral bureaucratic decision to abolish pensions between these two ages. It is also possible to imagine that these points will be picked up, by the trade unions in particular, and will be the subject of future parliamentary and extra-parliamentary debate, forcing the Ministry to clarify its intentions and take account of the other actors.

The strengths and weaknesses of national practice

Strengths: Periodic review, consultation and flexibility

1. Timing

The five-yearly "rendezvous" is certainly a major strength of the Japanese institutional arrangements. It means that the subject is almost continuously on the agenda, which avoids any debate on the relevance of carrying out a review (but does not, of course, prevent debate of reforms).

2. Flexibility

The continuous nature of the review of the pension schemes and the need, at least every five years, to review and, if necessary, reform them, encourages a constant search for original solutions, if not always proposing realistic measures. That applies to the last of the five scenarios in the White Paper: unrealistic, but stated, if only to stimulate further reflection.

3. Consensus

Historically, pension reform in Japan has not always been mere formality accompanied by a sense of resignation. When the basic system was created in 1959, the debate was long and lively, with heavy involvement of the social partners and the political parties.

Weaknesses: Guided consensus, bureaucracy and determinism

1. Reinforcing bureaucratic power in the reform process

It is clear that the Consultative Committee on Pensions is run by the Ministry of Health and Social Affairs. But the degree of control enjoyed by the civil servants leaves them open to the temptation to fence in the Committee's work, not only by managing appointments and reappointments (or non-reappointments), but by choosing the rapporteurs from the Committee and thus becoming de facto drafters of the report.

The publication of the White Paper, whose aim is to publicize the ministry proposals, completely excludes the Consultative Committee on Pensions and its work. It is perhaps a kind of tribute to the Committee whose work, despite bureaucratic management, does not perhaps sufficiently reflect the views of the Ministry, at least in its own eyes. The management of the process thus comes fully under the control of the Ministry, the content of the proposals being the last part of the process which ought to be a matter for the Committee (where the civil service is represented).

2. Justifications in the form of assumptions

The deterioration in the demographic balance is a fact, but the accounting scenarios are based on rather pessimistic demographic assumptions, extrapolating current trends over a long period and excluding any social change (notably concerning retirement age, women's employment rates or other factors). In addition, the scientific illusion of reliance on figures results in society and the economy being regarded as fixed, "other things being equal".

There is assumed to be a "tolerance threshold" for pension contributions, and according to the White Paper, this would be 30 per cent. How can one, in fact, foresee acceptance or rejection of rises in contributions?

3. Lack of proper debate

Apart from the reinforcement of bureaucratic power, the absence of public debate on pensions should be recognized. The social partners may naturally have divergent views, but the debate which could allow the public to see different sides based on the airing of little-known facts is not on the table.

4. Neglected issues

The method of managing reform may result in an absence of consideration of questions, which are important ones. The failure to resolve them may have an adverse impact on the position of future pensioners. Examples are the omission of the indexation issue and the fact that one-third of those in category 1, who are neither wage earners nor spouses of wage earners, do not pay contributions.

5. Additional observation

One of the important aspects rarely brought up is the organic link between the civil service and the ruling political party.

Regardless of the importance of a committee or the representative nature of some of the actors, the privileged relationship between civil servants and the Liberal Democratic Party, which introduces the bill in Parliament, remains the crucial linkage in the transition from reports containing proposals for reform and the drafting of a bill, presented by the LPD to Parliament.

Notes

[1] See table and data in Annex 1.

[2] It should be emphasized that one-third of the people in category 1 (neither wage earners nor spouses of wage earners; see below) do not contribute, because the universal compulsory contribution is voluntary in their case (and not a compulsory deduction).

[3] This method, which according to the Ministry of Health and Social Affairs is specific to Japan, has two synonymous names, which can be translated respectively as "adjusted capitalization method" or "graduated contribution method". But in presenting the method to the Japanese public, the Ministry uses the term "pay-as-you-go". The term "pay-as-you-go with reserves" was chosen here and applies to the following state schemes: the basic scheme, the compulsory supplementary scheme for private sector employees and the special schemes.

[4] Between age 60 and 65 years, the basic pension of 66,625 yen is covered by the employees' scheme. After age 65, the pension, in an identical amount, is covered under the basic regime. The proportional pension is paid from age 60, as an annuity, from the employees' scheme.

[5] See table and data in Annex 1.

[6] The LDP is still a major actor in Japanese politics. Since losing its majority in the Diet in 1993, it has had to share the lead with other members of coalitions on several occasions.

[7] In other words, management is not limited to the present, but tries to take into account the future position of the schemes.

[8] See list of members in Annex 2.

[9] A summary of earlier reforms is given in Annex 3.

[10] Although some small leaflets had previously been published, the 1998 publication was the first of its kind, and bore, moreover, the title of *White Paper on pensions*.

[11] At present, and only since 1994, bonuses are subject to a contribution of 1 per cent and are not taken into account in calculating benefits. Bonuses are a very common form of additional remuneration, and the Ministry assumes them to be 30 per cent on top of the basic monthly salary. Thus a contribution rate of 30 per cent on the basic monthly salary comes to $30/1.3 = 23$ per cent on an annual basis (the Ministry, in its calculation, ignores the contribution on the bonus).

Annex 1

Japanese pension schemes (at 31 March 1997)

	Contributors (millions of persons)		No. of schemes	Assets ($Y10^{12}$)
				235.6
	(10.6)	End-of-service benefits funded	90,000	18.5
	(12.1)	Pension funds	1,885	45.0
(0.91) 72 Non wage-earners' schemes	(33.0) 1 Compulsory employees' scheme	(5.8) 4 Special schemes		164.3
(70.2)	Basic pension (universal scheme)		1	7.8

Non wage earner	Wage earner	Wage-earners' spouses
(19.4)	(38.9)	(12.0)

Source: White Paper on pensions, 1998.

Pensions

	No. of schemes	Members (millions)	Beneficiaries (millions)	Average monthly contribution (Y)	Average monthly pension (Y)	Assets ($Y10^{12}$)
End-of-service	90 000	10.6	n.a.	–	n.a.	18.5
Pension funds	1 885	12.1	2.2	4 920	12 414	45.0
Special schemes	4	5.8	2.5	n.a.	219 000	45.0
Wage-earners' scheme	1	33.0	6.9	56 908	170 000	118.5
Non wage-earners' schemes	72	0.9	n.a.	19 212	73 000	0.8
Universal scheme	1	70.2	17.6	12 800	46 000	7.8
Total						235.6

Annex 2

Consultative Committee on Pensions of the Ministry of Health and Social Affairs

Name	Institution
FUKUOKA	President of the Japanese Federation of Company Directors (*Nikkeiren*)
ISAKODA	President of the Federation of Local Government Employees' Pension Funds
KIHARA	Vice-Chairperson, Shin Nihon Aciers Company
KÔSHIRO	Professor at the University of Ondes
KUBOTA	Vice-President of the Federation of Electrical Industries
KUNIHIRO	Professor of Social Sciences, Musashi University
KYÔGOKU	*Chairperson*, Professor Emeritus, University of Tokyo
MASUMOTO	Head of the Social Section of the Trade Union Federation (*Rengô*)
MEGURO	Professor at SOPHIA University
OKAZAKI	Former Professor of Law at the University of Nihon, former Director of the Centre for Population Research
SAKAMAKI	Professor in the Faculty of Social Sciences of Shokutoku University. Leader-writer on the *Maininchi* journal
TAKAYAMA	Professor at the Centre for Economic Research, University of Hitotsbashi
TOMITA	Director of the National Association of Local Authorities, Mayor of Yokose
TSUMURA	Professor in the Faculty of Economics, Chûkyô University
WAKASUGI	Executive Adviser to the Shin-Etsu Chemical Company
WATANABE	Adviser to the Association of Pension Actuaries of Japan
YAGI	*Vice-Chairperson*, President of the Association for Pension Funds Development (deceased)
YAMADA	Vice-President of the Central Association of Unions of Agricultural Mutual Insurance Associations
YAMANE	Vice-President of the Central Committee of the Federation of Chemical Workers' Trade Unions
YOSHIWARA	President of the Association of Pension Funds

Expert members

FUNAGÔ	President of the Federation of Special Pension Schemes
KAIZUKA	Professor in the Faculty of Law, Chûô University

Annex 3

Earlier reforms

1965-75: Development of the pension system and increase in benefits

During this period, while the pension system was being developed, all the political parties were in favour of an increase in benefits, in a context of rapid economic growth. Japan was becoming a major economic power again, but many Japanese, including politicians and journalists, as well as Japan's trading partners, regarded Japan's social security system, especially pensions, as inadequate.

The demographic ratio was also very favourable. The reference period for access to full entitlements was not very long, from 20 to 25 years depending on the case. The generations that retired during this period had had long careers, generally at least 40 years. The result was that some pensioners at that time enjoyed an earnings replacement rate higher than 100 per cent. When the level of maturity of the pension system increased, that formula for calculating pensions could not be maintained as it was.

Reform of 1985-86

During the completion stage, in 1985-86, a reform resulted in the first reduction in benefits. However, this did not meet any particular resistance, as a consensus emerged that the benefits were too generous. In addition, the 1986 reform introduced a first universal element, previously separate for private sector employees, civil servants and non wage earners.

Reform of 1994

During the forward-planning and proactive-management stage, in 1994, reform took place when the political party which had been in power for almost all the post-Second World War period had just lost the election and had been replaced by a coalition. However, the change did not have major significance, since the process of reform was mainly managed by the civil service.

The main effect of the 1994 reform was to reduce total benefits by raising the age at which wage earners were entitled to a full basic pension from 60 to 65 years, which was thus progressively brought in line with other categories. Other similar measures were taken, especially indexation of pensions no longer based on gross salary but on net salary, inspired by the 1992 reform in Germany. The increase in contributions was progressive, based on graduated growth, with a step of 2.5 per cent every five years, rising from 14 per cent to almost 30 per cent.

Sweden: Reform of the public pension system

6

*Eskil Wadensjö**

Sweden has recently made a major change in the public pension programme, the largest since the introduction of the present earnings-related pension scheme in 1960. The final decision on the new pension programme was taken by the Parliament (*Riksdag*) in June 1998, although some details remain unresolved. The new pension system will pay out the first pensions in the year 2001.

Decisions regarding the principles of the public pension programmes are taken by Parliament, but the outcome is influenced by other actors. Most important is the Government with its capacity to initiate investigations and make proposals to Parliament. Other actors such as political parties, trade unions and employers' associations also play an important role through their ability to form opinion and influence the decisions taken in Parliament.

This country study: (a) describes the present pension system; (b) discusses the political process leading to the pension reform of 1998; (c) provides an overview of the new pension system; (d) describes the transition from the old pension system to the new one; (e) presents the actors in the pension reform process and those involved in the day-to-day decisions taken by the pension authorities and the changes in the pension schemes between the major reforms; and (f) makes some comments on the strengths and weaknesses of Swedish pension practice.

The present pension system

Since 1960 the social security pension system in Sweden has consisted of two parts: a basic pension and a supplementary earnings-related pension. These two pensions together replace around 65 per cent of an individual's earnings (more

---

* Professor of Labour Economics, Swedish Institute for Social Research, University of Stockholm.

for those with low earnings) up to a ceiling. The pensions are indexed through calculation of a base amount which follows the consumer price index (for calculating social security pensions, a base amount is used which is presently reduced by 2 per cent). The base amount was in 1998 36,400 Swedish Krona.

The basic pension has been the same for everyone except in the case of married couples, where both receive old age pensions. The sum of their two pensions combined is less than twice that of a person who is not married to another person with an old-age pension. From 1993 a new requirement was introduced. To be eligible for a full basic pension, 40 years of residence in Sweden between the ages of 16 and 64 years, or 30 years of earnings, are required (only the years with earnings that amount to at least an entire base amount are included). If the requirements are not fulfilled, the pension is reduced proportionally.

To be eligible for a supplementary pension – the ATP pension – three years of paid employment are required, at least one with earnings equal to or higher than the base amount and for a full pension, 30 years, with earnings at the same level. The pension is based on the average of the 15 years with the highest (real) earnings. There is a ceiling of 7.5 base amounts. Earnings over 7.5 base amounts do not influence the size of the pension. Additional pension supplements and housing supplements are granted to those who have no supplementary pensions or a very low rate.

The retirement age was 67 from 1913 to 1 July 1976, and has been 65 since. A reduced early old-age pension or an enhanced late old-age pension have been options since 1960. At present it is possible to qualify for an early old-age pension from the age of 60, but delay the pension to the age of 70. The pension will also be reduced after age 65 if it is taken up before age 65. Since 1960 it has been possible to get a half old-age pension (with the reduction or enhancement calculated using the same principles as for a full pension). The age interval has been the same as for a full pension. Options of one-quarter and three-quarters old-age pensions have been available since July 1993.

Labour legislation gives job security in the form of seniority rules which apply to lay-offs up to the age of 67. It is possible for an employer to lay off a worker aged 67 or more with only one month's notice. The rules of the job security law can be changed by collective agreement, and in most cases the social partners have changed the age limit from 67 to 65 (mandatory retirement before age 67 is legal if an agreement has been reached by the social partners).

The disability pension forms part of the same system and has been calculated in the same way as the old-age pension except that the earnings in the years from retirement up to the age of 65 have been estimated for the calculation of the pension ("assumption points"). In 1970 it became possible to take labour market reasons together with medical reasons into account when granting a disability pension for people aged 63 or older (changed to 60 in 1976). In 1972 it became possible to grant a disability pension for labour market reasons only to people aged 63 or older (changed to 60 in 1974). In practice, this meant that people aged 63 (60 from 1974) who had exhausted their rights to receive unemployment compensation were disability pensioned. As the maximum period for unemployment compensation is one year and nine months for people aged 55 or more, those aged 58 years and three months who became unemployed could in practice "retire". This combination of payments from two income transfer systems was called "58.3-pensions". The granting of these "unemployment" pensions was discontinued from October 1991 when the granting of new disability pensions for labour market reasons was abolished. From January 1997 the possibility of getting a disability pension for combined medical and labour market reasons for older workers disappeared. Medical reasons are now the only valid criteria for granting a disability pension.

A special part-time pension system was introduced in 1976. The main requirements up to 1994 were that the applicant had to be between 60 and 65 years of age, working time had to be reduced by at least five hours a week, the remaining working time had to be at least 17 hours a week, and the person had to have been employed for at least ten years since the age of 45. In 1994 the earliest age for entitlement was raised from 60 to 61 and the maximum compensated number of hours was set at ten. The compensation rate was also lowered from 65 to 55 per cent.

A part-time pension is more favourable than a partial old-age pension because receiving a part-time pension does not reduce an old-age pension after the age of 65. A partial old-age pension acquired from the age of 60, for example, is reduced by 30 per cent in comparison with the old-age pension acquired at the age at 65, and the reduction continues after age 65.

The present pension system is a pay-as-you-go system but with partial funding of supplementary pensions and also a special fund for part-time pensions. The basic pension is financed out of the state budget but with a special contribution paid by the worker. Supplementary pensions are mainly financed from a payroll contribution and revenues from the funds. The AP-funds (the funds for the ATP pensions) amounted to 564 billion krona at the end of 1995.

The political process

The Swedish pension system has been the focus of an intense debate during the last two decades and several parliamentary and governmental committees have investigated all aspects of the system. The main worries have been that the decline in economic growth, longer life expectancy, increased frequency of disability pensioning and other forms of early exit from the labour market, and the pension financing of the baby-boom generation of the 1940s would have led to very high contributions in the first decades of the twenty-first century if the system had not been changed.

The old-age pension scheme was very difficult to change. There are several reasons for this. People's working lives are influenced by the pension system. Those who are currently working would have made other choices with another pension system. Changes in the pension system therefore had to be made in a way which would not alienate large groups of people who were already in the labour market (in other words, large groups of voters), especially those close to retirement age. Another factor was that the existing pension system was decided on in 1959 after an intense political conflict, including a referendum (the third of a total of five referendums in Sweden up to now) and an extra general election (the second extra general election, and the only one in the post-war period). The major political parties tried to avoid a political conflict of that type this time, but that also meant that the political process had to take longer.

A parliamentary committee that had examined this problem for several years presented its final report in 1990. The lively discussion and criticism of the committee's proposals resulted in a decision by the Government not to put forward a proposal for a change in the old-age pension system but instead to appoint a governmental committee comprised of members from all the political parties that were represented in Parliament. This committee presented a report in March 1994, with a proposal for a radically reformed pension system. The proposal was supported by the four liberal and conservative parties that formed the government at the time, and also the main opposition party – the Social Democratic Party. The Government presented proposed guidelines for a reform of the pension system based on the report. The proposal was accepted by Parliament in June 1994.

Only the general principles, and no legal changes, were decided on by Parliament in June 1994. A third committee (in a formal sense a working party) was appointed with members from the political parties in Parliament which supported the reform (the four liberal and conservative parties which formed the Government in 1991-94 and the Social Democratic Party). This committee worked to transform the guidelines into proposals for legislation. A first proposal was put forward in June 1995, but it did not lead to any decisions taken in Parliament. Several problems were still not solved. Instead the committee continued its work. Other committees were – and in some cases are still – working with some other issues related to changes in the pension system.

The debate within the Social Democratic Party on the principles of the pension reform was renewed in the spring of 1996. The Social Democratic Party Congress decided that the pension scheme had to be discussed anew inside the party. The local-level organizations of the party were asked to study the principles of the new pension scheme and give their opinions to the party secretariat no later than November 1996. The local-level organizations criticized some parts of the reform, especially the premium reserve part, as well as the employees' contributions and the lack of information regarding disability pensions. This led to a new round of negotiations on some parts of the pension reform between the five political parties who supported it. On 5 March 1997 it was announced that the political parties involved had reached an agreement regarding the premium reserve part. The proposal for the new system was presented to Parliament in spring 1998, and Parliament made its decision in June 1998.

The new pension system, whose principles had been decided by Parliament in June 1994, was to be implemented from 1 January 1996 as regards the payment of contributions and the accumulation of pension credits, with a minor exception. This date was later postponed three times to 1 January 1999. The first pensions in the new system will start to be paid in 2001.

The new pension system

The main idea behind the new pension system is to increase work incentives by providing for a closer linkage between an individual's contributions and pension entitlement, and thereby make the system viable from an actuarial point of view. The system is to become more an insurance system and less a system for income redistribution. A second aim of the reform is that the pension system should guarantee a basic income for everyone in old age. This means that some redistribution should take place, but it should be more visible than in the present system. The major change is the change from a defined benefit to a defined contribution system. This new defined contribution pension system is partly a pay-as-you-go system and partly a premium reserve system, with the pay-as-you-go system as the main part. The construction of the defined contribution pay-as-you-go system is an interesting innovation.

Pensions will be based on the individual's annual earnings for those aged 16 years or over, including earnings after the age of 65. An amount corresponding to 18.5 per cent of earnings will constitute the pension credits accrued during a year (the same as the contributions, see below), 16 per cent to a pay-as-you-go scheme (*inkomstpension*) and 2.5 per cent to a premium reserve scheme (*premiepension*). Besides earnings (including transfer payments in the form of unemployment or sickness benefits, etc.), military service, care of one's own children up to the age of 4, years of study (to some extent) and years in receipt of disability pensions, all give pension credits. In general, hypothetical earnings are calculated (for example, for those who are at home caring for their children) and pension credits corresponding to 18.5 per cent of the hypothetical earnings are added to the person's account. In the present ATP pension system the *pension points* are counted in base amounts and the base amount is adjusted according to the consumer price index. The *pension credits* in the new system are also indexed, but to the average incomes of workers aged 16 to 64 (and are included in the basis for calculation of the index for those who have a high enough income to earn pension credits).

Transfer payments are taxable and therefore earn pension credits. However, unemployment and sickness benefits, sick-leave and so on are compensated at less than 100 per cent which leads to lower pension rights than for a person who is working. To compensate for the loss of pension credits, credits corresponding to 13.3 per cent of the transfer payments will be added to the accumulated credits. This means that if the replacement rate is 75 per cent, pension credits will be calculated on a sum corresponding to a 85 per cent replacement rate. There will be a ceiling on the income which is included in the calculation of pension credits. This ceiling will be 7.5 base amounts in 2000 and from 2001 will be based on an income index and not to the consumer price index, as in the present system.

Each year the accumulated pension credits of those who have reached age 65 that year are converted to a pension. This is done by using a partition rate, decided anew for every cohort upon reaching age 65. The size of the partition rate, and therefore the pension, depends on the expected period for which those who turn 65 will receive a pension. As the remaining life expectancy increases with each cohort, the partition rate will gradually increase, and therefore pensions will be lower for each cohort given the pension credits accumulated. (The calculation will be made every year using an equation determined by the law and will not be a political decision).

Secondly, there will also be a "guarantee-pension" (*garantipension*) for those with low or no earnings. For a full guarantee pension, the applicant must have lived in Sweden for at least 40 years between 16 and 65 years of age. A full guarantee pension is 2.1 base amounts for an unmarried pensioner and 1.87 base amounts for a married pensioner. The guarantee pension is reduced if the pensioner receives an earnings-related old-age pension. If the total pension is 3.0 or more base amounts for an unmarried pensioner or 2.655 base amounts or more for a married pensioner, the pension will consist of only the earnings-related component. How these pensions develop over time will depend on an index, but reduced by 1.6 per cent a year.

The new pensions will be financed by contributions amounting to 18.5 per cent of earnings. The present funds of the AP-scheme will also be used to finance pensions. As mentioned earlier, not only earnings but also military service, child care and so on will earn pension credits. The State will pay contributions to cover the pension credits acquired in this way. These contributions are calculated and paid in the same way as other contributions, the only difference being that it is the State, not the individual, that pays. The cost of the guarantee pensions will be funded from the state budget.

The system will be mainly pay-as-you-go, but part of it will be a premium reserve system: a contribution of 16 per cent is paid to the pay-as-you-go system, and 2.5 per cent to the premium reserve system. Payments to the premium reserve system of 1 per cent by the employee already started from the fiscal year 1995.

The present plan is that half the contributions will be paid by the employer and half by the employee. At present, supplementary pensions are financed by employers' contributions. However, the new system will most likely be implemented in the following way: the employees' contributions will be raised to 9.25 per cent of earnings in one step; at the same time the wage rate will be increased by the same percentage; the employers' contribution will be decreased to 9.25 per cent (it is higher in the present ATP scheme). Thus neither employees nor employers should gain or lose from the change in financing system. The idea behind converting employers' contributions into employees' contributions is that employees will be made more aware that they are gaining the right to a pension by paying for it, and therefore work incentives should be strengthened.

An employers' contribution of 9.25 per cent will be paid on the share of earnings exceeding 7.5 base amounts, but this payment will not be a basis for calculating the pension. The idea is that the adoption of the new pension scheme should not change the income distribution in the favour of those with the highest incomes.

A much discussed feature of the new pension scheme is the premium reserve element. This is the part of the new pension scheme that has already started. As mentioned earlier, a contribution corresponding to 1 per cent of the salary has been paid to the premium reserve scheme since 1995. Since the system is not functioning yet, these contributions are paid to the *Riksgäldskontoret* (the National Debt Office), which administers them. When the premium reserve scheme starts, the *Riksgäldskontoret* will transfer the accumulated contributions (including interest) to the financial institutions which will be responsible for investing the funds.

According to a proposal by a special committee that presented a report in summer 1996, the premium reserve part will be regulated in the following way:

1. The individual will decide which company he or she wishes to administer savings in the premium reserve part. Insurance companies, banks and newly founded institutions will be likely alternatives. Companies owned by the government will also be set up. The savings of those who do not select a specific company will be administered by *Riksförsäkringsverket* (the National Social Insurance Board). *Riksförsäkringsverket* is obliged to select

low-risk placements (which at the same time probably means lower returns on average). The other companies will also spread the risks, but may place the savings in riskier holdings than *Riksförsäkringsverket* is permitted to do (the same rules as for other government funds).

2. The company administering the savings must be approved and supervised by *Finansinspektionen* (the Financial Inspection Authority).
3. In case of death, the savings will be transferred to the relatives of the deceased.
4. It will be possible to begin claiming the pension from the age of 61. At the time of receiving the pension, the money is transferred to a governmental pension company which will administer the premium reserve pension.

The pension fund of the premium reserve scheme will gradually increase. When the system reaches maturity, its reserves will correspond to 25-30 per cent of GDP. That is about the same as the funds in the ATP scheme at present.

Married couples, where both of the spouses were born in 1954 or later, are offered the possibility of dividing their pension rights in the premium reserve part of the new system. Such a possibility does not exist in the present ATP scheme. A requisite is that both spouses apply and that the application is made before 31 January of the year in which both spouses want to divide their pension credits. Other requirements for a division of pension credits are that both spouses reside in Sweden and that neither of them receive an old-age pension. In the 1994 plan the intention was that it should be possible for spouses to divide all pensions credits accrued in a year. Several problems led to a change to a less ambitious plan.

After the application is made, the dividing of the pension credits continues until an application is made for a discontinuance or the couple divorces. If the couple mutually applies for a discontinuance, it becomes valid from the year of application. If only one of the spouses applies, it becomes valid from the year after the application. A discontinuance does not influence the pension credits that are already divided. They are divided permanently and it is not possible to transfer them back.

The change to actuarial pensions is intended to increase labour supply and delay retirement. Other steps have been taken with the same intention. Earlier, a reduced old-age pension could be received from the age of 60, but in the new pension system 61 will be the lowest age (this change will take place from 1999). On early retirement, the pensioner will receive only the earnings-related pension. A guarantee pension will only be possible from the age of 65.

The committee proposed that job security according to labour market legislation should be changed so that collective agreements could not influence the age limit, and that this limit should be raised first to age 66 and later to age 67. A proposal for a change in the labour market legislation has not been put forward yet. However, the Government expects the social partners to change their collective agreements of their own accord, and only if they do not will it propose that Parliament should change the job security law.

The part-time pension system, which has been the most popular way of combining work and retirement between the ages of 60 and 65, will be abolished. No new part-time pensions will be granted from the year 2000. The remaining combination of work and retirement in that age group will be partial old-age pensions from the age of 61 or over (the earnings-related part). As in the present pension system, it will be possible to draw one-quarter, a half and three-quarters of an old-age pension.

The transition from the present system to the new one

The pensions of those born in 1954 or later will be completely based on the new system. According to the proposal, the pensions of those born between 1935 and 1953 would be based on both systems. For those born in 1935, pensions would be based on the old system by 19/20 parts and on the new system by 1/20 parts for those born in 1936, 18/20 parts on the old system and 2/20 parts on the new system and so on. For those born between 1935 and 1953 there would be a special guarantee that the pension would never be lower than the entitlements under the ATP scheme, with the pension points accrued before 1995. For those born in 1934 or earlier, pensions would be completely based on the old system. On 18 April 1997, the five political parties represented in the committee agreed that those born in 1937 and earlier (and also those born in 1935, 1936 and 1937) would follow the old scheme.

To be able to calculate the new pensions for those who entered the labour market before 1997, the pension points acquired in the ATP scheme have to be translated into pension credits in the new scheme. This is done by adding one base amount (for the basic pension) to the base amounts gained in the ATP scheme and thereafter converting them to pension credits and using the same indexation as in the new pension scheme. The pension credits for child care will be calculated from 1960 onwards, the pension credits for military service and studies from 1995, and for other non-earnings based credits from 1997.

The pension for those who were born in 1937 or earlier will be completely based on the old system. However, there will be a specific guarantee for those with low pensions. If the new guarantee pension gives a higher pension than the present basic pension (including supplement) and the national supplementary pension, this group will receive a guarantee pension.

One important issue which remains to be settled is how to organize disability pensions. According to the guidelines laid down by Parliament, the disability pension system will no longer be part of the same system as the old-age pension system. A special committee investigated how to change that system and presented its results in July 1996. Its proposal is that the disability pension should be changed to a system with monthly compensation paid to those who received sickness benefits for one year and where the possibility of a return to work during a period of at least one year is deemed very small. The compensation will be based either on the average of four of the last six years' earnings (the year with the highest and the year with the lowest earnings will not be counted) or the average of all years from the age of 16 (excluding the five years with lowest income). The compensation level will be 65 per cent of the amount calculated. There are some points to be investigated as regards the disability pension scheme, especially on how to make the transition from the present scheme to the new one. A new investigation was started in spring 1997 on the design of the new scheme, and a report was presented later in 1997. The general principles were accepted by Parliament in March 1998.

There are still some problems to solve before the laws regulating the new disability pension scheme are complete. Some of the major issues still unresolved are as follows:

1. The mix of employers' and employees' contributions is not determined yet and the problems in connection with (the partial) switching from employers' to employees' contributions have not been solved.
2. There are considerable problems in collecting information and constructing schedules of conditions other than earnings that give pension rights.
3. The design of the disability pension scheme is still not decided on, but the general principles were agreed on in 1998.

The actors in the pension reform process and changes in the pension schemes

Progress towards a new pension system began with the Social Democratic Government appointing a special committee in November 1984. The under-secretary of the Ministry of Social Affairs was appointed chairperson. The under-secretary of a ministry is politically appointed and is second in command after the minister. Seven members of the committee besides the chairperson were appointed, three representing the Social Democratic Party and four representing each of the four other political parties in Parliament (but outside the Government): *Moderaterna* (the Conservative Party), *Folkpartiet* (the Liberal Party), *Centerpartiet* (the Centre Party, earlier the Farmers' Party) and *Vänsterpartiet* (the former Communist Party). Five of the seven were members of Parliament, meaning that all political parties in Parliament were represented.

In addition to the members, two categories of experts were appointed: *sakkunniga* and *experter*. Those belonging to the first category, *sakkunniga*, are appointed for the work as a whole and have more or less the same position as the members, but not as representatives of political parties. The members of the second category, *experter*, assist the committee in specific areas of competence. Both categories have the right to write minority reports and make reservations against all or parts of the recommendations of the committee.

Persons from three major trade union confederations – LO (blue-collar), TCO (white-collar) and SACO (university educated) – were appointed as *sakkunniga*. Additional *sakkunniga* were representatives from the major employers' associations for the private sector (SAF) and for the municipalities, the two major organizations of retired people, the federation of disability organizations, three ministries (Finance, Labour, Social Affairs), the National Social Insurance Board and LO's research institute. *Experter* were appointed from LO, TCO, SACO, SAF and the National Social Insurance Board. Researchers were commissioned to write special reports for the committee.

As seen from this listing of members and experts, all political parties in Parliament, the major social partners and groups with a special interest in the pension scheme were involved in the committee's work. One intention with committees of this type is to try to settle the issues inside the committee and present a proposal which could be accepted by a wide majority of Parliament.

Four committee reports were published in 1986, 1987, 1988 and 1989 on special aspects of the pension system (for example, widows'/widowers' pensions and the part-time pension system). The final report with a proposal for changes in the old-age pension scheme was presented in 1990. Several reservations and (minor) minority reports were included. Just as with other government reports, it was sent out to organizations, public authorities and so on to gather their opinions. The reactions were critical in many cases, and the Government decided not to put forward a proposal to Parliament but to appoint a new committee to find a solution.

The second committee was appointed in November 1991 by the liberal-conservative Government which had come to power after the September election. The Minister was appointed chairperson, an appointment which indicated the great importance of the committee. The other members represented the now seven parties in Parliament. This time experts were taken only from the Ministries of Finance and Social Affairs, and from the National Social Security Board, but not from the social partners. As in the former study, researchers were commissioned for reports.

The recommendations in the final report, published in March 1994, were supported by the members of the committee belonging to five of the political parties – the four parties forming the Government and the Social Democratic

Party. The representatives of two other parties were against the proposal and voiced reservations. These two parties were *Vänsterpartiet* and *Ny Demokrati*, a right-wing party represented in Parliament between 1991 and 1994.

The principles of the proposal were accepted by a large majority of Parliament in June 1994 but, as mentioned above, many problems were still not solved. A new committee, in a formal sense a working group inside the Ministry of Social Affairs, was appointed on 23 June 1994. Only members of the five parties in favour of the reform were appointed. This was possible as it was not a parliamentary or a governmental committee in a formal sense but only a working group. The Minister of Social Affairs was appointed chairperson of the committee.

The election in September 1994 meant a change from a liberal-conservative to a social democratic government. The new Social Democratic Minister of Social Affairs was appointed chairperson of the working group, but it continued to consist of the same five political parties as before the election. Two parties represented in Parliament were outside the committee, *Vänsterpartiet* and *Miljöpartiet* (the Green Party), the latter represented in Parliament after the 1994 election. Both these parties outside the working group were against the new pension scheme.

The results of the election in September 1998 meant a weakening of the representation of the Social Democratic party in Parliament. It formed the Government alone, but had to reach an agreement with other parties. It reached such an agreement regarding the state budget and other issues with the *Vänsterpartiet* and *Miljöpartiet* (in a red-green coalition in support of the Government). The pension reform, however, is outside the agreement and the old agreement between the five political parties is still the basis for that agreement.

As seen from this discussion, the pension reform started as a broad political investigation involving the social partners and other groups. At a later stage, it involved mainly the political parties of Parliament, and at the third and final stage only the political parties in favour of the pension reform.

The influence of the social partners has gradually declined, at least in so far as they are formally involved in the government committees. On the other hand, they have been important as lobbyists throughout, in some cases in close cooperation with the political parties involved. In one aspect of reform – pension financing – discussion and conflicts between unions and employers had delayed the political process. Agreement has been reached that contributions should correspond to 18.5 per cent of wages, but there are two points of contention: Should they be paid by employers or by employees? And if they are to be paid by the employee and not by the employer, as in the present ATP scheme, what should be the transitional arrangements (how should wages be increased to compensate wage earners)? It should also be noted that collectively bargained occupational pension schemes are important in Sweden – they cover almost everyone employed – and that those systems are decided on by the social partners through central agreements.

The "Swedish model" of industrial relations started with an agreement in 1938 between SAF (the private sector employers' federation) and LO (the organization of blue-collar unions): the Saltsjöbaden agreement. At that time blue-collar workers who worked in the private sector made up around 75 per cent of all employees in the economy. LO had very close links to the Social Democratic Party and SAF gave economic support to *Moderaterna* (the Conservative Party) and *Folkpartiet* (the Liberal Party). (TCO and SACO were not established yet, even if some rather small white-collar unions existed.) At that time LO could "deliver the votes" to the Social Democratic party in the elections (i.e. the majority of its members voted for that Party), and the Social Democratic Party, for its part, was very sensitive to the demands of LO. Changes in the labour market structure – a larger share of white-collar workers and a larger share working in the public sector – has led to a fall in the proportion of blue-collar workers employed in the private sector (the SAF-LO area of negotiations), which now comprise only 25 per cent of all employees. LO also organizes workers in the public sector, but TCO and SACO together now have almost as many members as LO, and the trend is in favour of the two white-collar organizations. SACO and TCO are not allied to any of the political parties and the votes of their members are not concentrated on a specific political party. More importantly, the votes of LO members are not so concentrated on the Social Democratic Party as before. This means that the party cannot rely mainly on votes from LO members in elections. Its relations with LO have been less close and the influence of LO less important.

So far we have presented the major pension reform and the process leading up to it. But there have also been a lot of piecemeal reforms. They are also decided by Parliament after a proposal by the Government, based on discussion in and recommendations from the standing social security committee of Parliament, as are all social security reforms, including the present pension reform. For minor reforms, those authorities have a greater influence than they have on major reforms which largely involve the political parties.

The present system of state governance in Sweden was decided upon as early as 1634 (public administration was reorganized as a response to the strains caused by Sweden's participation in the Thirty Years' War; Sweden entered the war in 1630, so the rather special structure of the Swedish system of public administration is more than 350 years old). The system is built on several influential boards, for example the National Labour Market Board, which (given the laws decided by Parliament) formulates detailed rules and takes decisions regarding specific cases. In the area of social security, there is a National Social Security Board

(*Riksförsäkringsverket*, RFV). A board is headed by a General Director, in this case a former (Social Democratic) Minister of Social Affairs. The other eight members of the Board are members of Parliament, representing the various political parties and the main trade unions, and a professor of social sciences.

The National Social Security Board is the authority that supervises the social security administration and issues guidelines (which in practice means interpreting the social security law). The social security administration, however, is organized for historical reasons by independent social security societies, one for each county. These are not part of the National Social Security Board, whereas, for example, the county labour market boards are part of the national labour market administration and are subordinated to the National Labour Market Board. The social security societies form a national organization, *Försäkringskasseförbundet* (FKF). Even this organization has board members that represent the political parties. The two organizations – RFV and FKF – compete in many respects. It is important to stress here that representatives of the political parties form the majority of both these organizations. A government report in 1996 proposed that the societies should become regional parts of the National Social Security Board, but no decision was taken. The influence of regional interests was most likely the cause.

Strengths and weaknesses of Swedish pension practice

The main strength of the Swedish system of pension reform is that it involves many actors; for example, the political parties in Parliament are involved in the process. They are involved on several levels, which means that many politicians are well informed about the social security system. The tendency to try to find broad compromises also leads to stability in the system. Changing majorities after a general election normally do not lead to the reversal of a decision taken beforehand. It is important to note the growing importance of the political parties in the process of changing the pension system. The most likely factor behind that development is that the labour force is now more equally split among the three top trade union federations, and the influence of the largest federation, LO, has therefore declined.

The main weakness with the system is that it takes time. The forthcoming problems in the present pension scheme were already well known in the early 1980s, after a decade of low growth compared to that of the 1960s. But it took ten years from the appointment of the first committee to reach a decision in Parliament on the main principles, and four more years for Parliament to adopt laws regulating the new pension scheme.

The public pension system in Italy: Observations on the recent reforms, methods of control and their application

7

Massimo Antichi* and Felice Roberto Pizzuti**

Introduction

Since the latter half of the 1970s, it was already clear to observers and experts in the sector that the Italian pension system needed structural changes. However, it was only in 1992, after much fruitless debate during the 1980s, that the reform was launched by the Amato Government, then continued[1] in 1995 by the Dini Government and in 1997 by the Prodi Government.

The reform was rendered necessary not only by worsening sectoral problems and their increasingly unsustainable social and economic impact, but also, and to a far from insignificant extent, by some major overall economic and political changes that occurred in the 1990s.

Among the new features of the economic and political scene in the early 1990s, which can help explain the shift from the long period of fruitless debate to the phase of implementating reforms, were the turning point in 1992 in economic policy with the devaluation of the lira and Italy's exit from the European Monetary System (EMS); the political upheavals and economic effects of the resultant continuing instability; and the fact that politicians and trade unions began to show greater maturity in their attitudes to the means and objectives of economic policy, social policy and social security.

The influence of the new economic and political climate on pension reform in the 1990s

Following the devaluation of the lira and the traumatic exit from the EMS in the summer of 1992, and thus after Italy lost an instrument of monetary discipline

* Costs Evaluation Unit, Ministry of Labour and Social Security.

**Department of Government Economics, Faculty of Economic Science, La Sapienza University, Rome.

– the cost of which had proved unsustainable for the economy – restrictive budgetary policy (in particular cuts in public expenditure) was recognized as the principal instrument which would in future have to be used to defend the credibility of the Italian economy in international financial markets.

On the issue of old-age provision, at the same time as the emergency budgetary restrictions adopted after the devaluation, the Amato Government, without the public or even the trade unions fully realizing it, introduced changes which, for the same level of contributions, taking into account all the effects on the system, would have meant a considerable reduction in retirement pensions. What remained unchanged, on the other hand, were numerous, serious anomalies in the system, in both technical terms and equity. These were essentially due to the coexistence of a proliferation of different pension schemes operating in a way that discriminated either between different categories of private sector employees, between the latter and the public sector, or between employees in both sectors and the self-employed.

Assuming, for example, constant growth in GDP of 2 per cent per annum and, for each employee, an average additional increase, in respect of seniority, of 1 per cent, a private sector employee with 35 years' contributions, who would formerly have received a pension replacing about 66 per cent of final salary, would only have received, under the proposed Amato reform, about 47 per cent of final salary, a reduction of almost 30 per cent.

The change with the greatest consequences was the abolition of indexation of pensions to growth in real earnings. Under the new system, 15 years after a worker's retirement, his or her initial pension lost 35 per cent of its value relative to current salaries.[2] Using the previous example, under the scheme proposed by the Amato Government, the relation between pensions and current salaries, 15 years after retirement, would have fallen from 47 per cent to about 30 per cent.

The approval of the Amato reform was made easier by two measures whose principle was reproduced in the 1995 reform. First, the changes were made without touching the most visible elements of the current scheme, such as the multiplier of 2 per cent per annum used to calculate the pension, and the entitlement to an old-age pension after 35 years' contributions. Second, the hidden cuts, substantial though they were, such as those linked to the limitation of pension indexing, were introduced gradually, so as not to be felt immediately but later, in stages.

When about a year later, people began to realize the implications of the changes of the Amato reforms, the Ciampi Government took the view that the effects of the measures taken by its predecessor needed to be mitigated. It raised the reference salary used to calculate pensions by eliminating from the calculation the lowest salaries corresponding to a maximum of 25 per cent of working life.[3] This meant a "recovery" of about half the pension reduction which would have occurred under the Amato reform.

The March 1994 elections and the resulting Berlusconi Government marked a very significant stage in modern political development in Italy. Among other things, there were obvious effects on the positions of the various political parties and social actors in the debate on economic and social security policy.

The worsening and prolongation of political uncertainty led to a deterioration in the situation in so far as the pressures exerted in the Italian economy by international markets were concerned.

Between 1994 and 1995, the uncertainty and surprise caused by the new political balance led the trade unions and the forces of the centre-left, who found themselves in opposition, also to review their positions on social security, in the hope that this might perhaps help reverse the political situation – which is what did in fact happen.

After the fall of the Berlusconi Government, as a result of strong social opposition to its proposed deep cuts in pensions provision – and faced with the clear necessity to make radical changes to the existing system – the Dini Government, the new centre-left majority and the trade unions agreed to work together in the field of pensions. However, because of various differences of approach, some a matter of form and others of substance, the new reform contained major elements of continuity in relation to the route traced by the Amato Government.

Pension reform: Law No. 335 of 8 August 1995 (the Dini reform)

The fundamental innovation of the Dini reform, compared with the previous pension system, and the measures taken to harmonize the benefits of the different existing schemes, was that it had not only economic and financial effects, but also effects on the equity of the pension system.

Law 335/95 was undoubtedly the culmination of the reform process launched by the Amato law in 1992, but it also represented, within the new system, a parameter whereby it became possible to evaluate the consistency of successive legislation.

One can gain a better appreciation of the innovative nature, the objectives and the limitations of the 1995 reform by setting it in the context of the legislative process applying to the pension system.

The quotation from article 38[4] of the Constitution found in the 1995 Reform Act and the following declaration that the provisions of the Act "constitute fundamental principles of the economic and social reform of the Republic", as well as their purely proclamatory value, define very clearly the legislator's intention to make structural changes designed to impose basic general and uniform rules, with a view to overall expansion of public social security.[5]

The most significant aspects of the 1995 reform can be summarized as follows:

- adoption, as the method for calculating benefits under the new system, of a defined contribution system which, because it is a pay-as-you-go public scheme, respects the principles of solidarity to which Italian compulsory pension provision has historically been attached. Moreover, it provides for a closer relationship between contributions and benefits, especially as the amount is also determined on the basis of the age of retirement or the average life expectancy from the time when the pension is paid;
- convergence of different types of pension provision on the general scheme for employees in the private sector (*Fondo Pensioni Lavoratori Dependenti, FPLD*), which is taken as the general reference model for the pension system. This is achieved by a progressive alignment or harmonization of the various existing schemes, keeping as separate schemes only those whose special nature is justified by its particular objectives and the needs of the specific occupational sectors concerned. In the future, this will remove many of the impediments to workers' mobility caused by the diversity of existing pension schemes;
- raising of the age at which a retirement pension can be drawn and abandoning the system of seniority in favour of a single retirement pension (which thus replaces retirement pensions, early retirement pensions and seniority pensions). This pension, while following the actuarial rules to determine the amount of benefit payable, also allows a degree of flexibility in the conditions of access, based on individual choice, of course, but also on the demands of the labour market;
- revision of the system of occupations considered as "arduous", now defined as a special situation of a general nature (i.e. concerning in each pension scheme a significant proportion of the insured, such as entertainment workers), which can result in early access to the retirement pension;
- extension of compulsory pension insurance, on the one hand, by providing certain types of retirement pension to the liberal professions which were previously outside the scope of compulsory insurance and, on the other, by creating an appropriate separate administration, within the National Institute for Social Security (INPS), to which so-called "para-employees"[6] belong;
- emphasis on the separation of benefits of a strictly "insurance" nature and provisions of an "assistance" kind by social insurance institutions, so as to clearly define their respective sources of financing;
- increased development of complementary forms of pension provision as a compensating instrument to restore pension levels.

The reform hinges primarily on the return to the principle of solidarity, under which the pension system must apply to all workers as uniformly as possible, by abolishing all the different rules which, unless they are justified on objective grounds, amounted to as many privileges. This objective is a prerequisite for the introduction of a single pension system (apart from the separate schemes which are justified on the grounds of real and continuing peculiarities). It must be achieved by stages[7] and, for harmonizing the different pension schemes in existence, will essentially involve adopting decrees for the purpose.

The legislative measures taken completely remodelled the existing system, but did so progressively, because of: (a) the diversity of situations, which sometimes required treatment on a case-by-case basis; (b) the implications for contributions and thus labour costs; (c) the obligation to take into account the expectations of those affected, reinforced by previous rules, and thus to adopt a pro rata method;[8] and (d) the need, linked to the foregoing, to regulate retirement from the labour market, there too taking into account the process of restructuring and changes in the manufacturing base.

The second fundamental principle of the reform is undoubtedly strict respect for balance in pensions management. This is guaranteed by the option adopted for calculating pensions due: the defined contribution system ensures a closer linkage between benefits and contributions and is supported by a mechanism which allows prior determination of the rate of return on pensions, strictly linked to fluctuations in GDP.

Because it maintains the pay-as-you-go system, which is in any case imposed by the considerable "stock" of pensioners as of 31 December 1995, the new defined contribution method of calculation is an innovation compared with the previous system. With the new method, pension contributions paid by workers during their working life are accumulated by a process of indexed capitalization at the rate of growth of national monetary income. Then, at the date of retirement, the accumulated capital is repaid in line with the insured person's life expectancy, applying a conversion factor which varies according to the age of retirement. The conversion factor may be adjusted every ten years.[9] The old-age pension paid is also calculated by the up-front application of a discount rate of 1.5 per cent.[10]

By making the correlation between the amount of pension paid out and the contributions paid even closer, the defined contribution system, in the sense that its aim is to make the system economically viable, is an essential instrument to restore the financial equilibrium sought by the reform. The defined benefit system's calculation formula, which bases the amount of pension on the final salary, involves rates of return that have almost no relation to trends in the national economy.

Indeed, the defined benefit system, apart from the fact that it means applying rates of return that are financially unsustainable because they are higher than the growth rate of the contributions intended to finance pensions, is unfair to the beneficiaries, in that the rates of return offered by the pension system differ depending on which pension scheme one belongs to, one's age and one's final salary.[11]

In the defined contribution system, under the principle of equivalence between benefits and contributions, the system that allowed entitlement to the statutory minimum pension is superseded, since from now on to be entitled to a pension before reaching age 65, the contributions paid must provide a pension equal to at least 1.2 times the social pension (which is about 7.5 million lira, adjusted each year based on the price index).[12]

The 1995 reform is ultimately a reform that is characterized by a return towards the social insurance model, with better adherence to the principle of equivalence between contributions and benefits.[13] This is despite the persistence of features of the previous schemes (maintenance of the pay-as-you-go system, the proportion between pensions and earned income, the minimum pension, etc.), which can be considered rather as expressions of the principle of solidarity than characteristics that contradict the new model.

From the point of view of the financial consequences, the fact that Law 335/95 chose the defined contribution system for calculating pensions is clearly important. Apart from the exceptions mentioned earlier, it shows the correlation between contributions and benefits in a transparent manner. But the same degree of equivalence could have been achieved by adopting measures which, under the distributive system, would have had the aim of basing the benefit calculations not on contributions paid during the last years of work, but on those paid throughout the working life.

The most important innovation introduced by the reform, still in terms of financial consequences, is the indexation of the notional rate of return for pensions, calculated in advance and indissolubly linked to fluctuations in GDP. This means very strict control of the pension rate of return, so that it is always aligned with changes in the income on which contributions are payable (and thus changes in contributions themselves) and GDP, by making periodic adjustments either to the rate of capitalization (rate of revaluation of contribution annuities making up the total notional individual contribution), or to the conversion factors (derived from the average life expectancy for men and women, for the corresponding age groups).

The slowdown in the rate of increase of pension expenditure is obtained in the following way: (a) freezing of the percentage used to calculate the amount of pension under the defined contribution system (33 per cent of income subject to contributions for employees and 20 per cent of income subject to contributions for the self-employed); (b) application of a ceiling on salary or income subject to contributions; (c) stricter rules concerning the aggregation of employment income and pension benefit, and for pensions based on "seniority" which remain in force for those who have worked for over 40 years; (d) application of an income condition for granting a survivors' pension; and (e) payment of a single disability pension of the same amount based on the beneficiary's condition and not on the cause of the disability.

Also with respect to financial consequences, the process of harmonizing the many existing pension schemes will not only allow a rationalization inspired by the principles of equity already described, but will also restore financial stability to the various fund managements in the context, as already seen, of convergence.

Law 335/95 extends and reinforces the integral development of the regulations on complementary pensions, introduced by legislative decree No.124 of 21 April 1993.

Provisions subsequent to Law 335/95, in particular Law 449/97

Following the Dini reform in 1995, as the needs for reform changed and became more and more urgent, the pension system very quickly became the subject of lively debate and controversy, with the proposed adoption of measures which, in the context of a wholesale restructuring of the Welfare State, would bring expenditure on social security under control. Preceded and accompanied by the now traditional measures for closing off access to seniority pensions, the provisions of the Finance Act, Law 449/97, were the fruit of those debates.

This law, by its scope and the importance of the welfare issues it covers, is a natural successor to the 1995 reform, which it amplifies and complements by accelerating and reinforcing the process of harmonization of retirement pensions. This is the tenor of its main provisions, which are set out below:

- amendment of the conditions for awarding seniority pensions; in particular, the new provisions swept away the so-called "baby-pensions" in the public sector, by aligning public sector pensions much more closely with the private sector;
- application to all beneficiaries of defined benefits paid in addition to the statutory pension or incorporated in it – in order to obtain this pension – of the provisions of the general compulsory pension scheme concerning access and effective dates;

- acceleration of the transition phases to achieve the full application of the conditions on civil status and contributions under certain special schemes which enjoy special treatment;
- raising the percentages of contributions for the self-employed: artisans, traders and self-employed farmers;
- alignment of contribution percentages for the various types of substitution retirement pensions managed by the INPS, whenever they are lower than those applicable to the vast majority of the self-employed; and
- application of the same treatment to employees and the self-employed relating to accumulation of a retirement pension and self-employed income.

Among the provisions whose nature related rather to the economic situation, and which affected the level of expenditure, mention should be made of those concerning the freezing – total in 1998 and partial for the following three years – of the automatic indexing of the highest retirement pensions to the cost of living. The legislator clearly considered these pensions as substantial enough to be able to bear this measure without excessively attacking their adequacy to the beneficiaries' needs, as provided for and protected in the Constitution.

The role of the Government, institutions and social actors in the process of pension reform

In Italy, bills (draft legislation) are introduced either by Parliament or by the Government. For a law to be passed, it must be ratified in the same form by the two chambers of Parliament (the Chamber of Deputies and the Senate of the Republic). Only in cases of necessity or emergency, which are decided by the President of the Republic, may the Government take a measure (decree) which enters immediately into force. The validity of this measure, however, is subject to a time limit. If the decree is not converted into a law (or approved by the two chambers) within 60 days, it becomes immediately void (or retroactively from the date of its promulgation).

The Government may, however, be empowered by Parliament, which adopts for the purpose a law defining the criteria, the guiding principles and the time limit, to take a measure which has the force of law (legislative decree). In such cases, Parliament's approval is no longer necessary. Parliament only has to give an opinion on whether or not the Government has respected the criteria laid down, but that opinion is not binding on the executive. Only the Constitutional Court, if application is made, has the right to raise objections to the measure taken. It is thus impossible to attribute full powers or permanent legislative powers to the Government on a particular issue.

The routes chosen for the adoption of the most recent measures to reform the Italian pension system have been very varied. It should first be explained that the participation of the social partners in the reform process is not institutionalized. As indicated earlier, the launch of the Amato reform in 1992 was not the outcome of any of the debates that had occurred in the previous ten years, but was the result of the worsening economic situation due to the pressing monetary problems which led to the devaluation of the lira and the exit from the EMS. The legislative procedure followed on that occasion also showed the exceptional character of the circumstances of the time, which required sending clear and timely signals to the international financial markets that Italy was able to regain control of its public expenditure. The Government was, in fact, empowered by Parliament to reform the pension system. This gave the Amato Government an instrument which conferred on it a contractual advantage over the social partners, especially the trade unions.

The process of correction of the Dini draft reform which preceded its adoption is, on the other hand, much more difficult to analyse. After the Amato reform, the provisions on the contribution percentages needed to achieve financial equilibrium produced by the actuarial section of the INPS, the main state pension body – which managed about two-thirds of all pensions currently being paid – and by the National Accounts Service *(Ragionera Generale dello Stato)*, showed that the Amato reform would not be able to rein in pension costs in the medium term and bring them in line with what was manageable at the macroeconomic level. Employers and government officials both realized the need to adopt a new set of measures to fill what was unanimously seen as the most serious gap in the 1992 reform: the failure to correct the development of seniority pensions and thus to continue awarding pensions solely on the basis of having paid contributions for a period of 35 years.

To try and reach a consensus on the measures needed, the centre-right coalition Government, led by Silvio Berlusconi, which had won the 1994 elections, appointed an expert commission in the summer of 1994, headed by Professor Castellino, with the task of drawing up proposed corrections to the pension system for inclusion in the Finance Act for the three-year period 1995–97. This was to be introduced in Parliament, for adoption, at the end of September 1994.

Apart from the members appointed by the Government, the Commission included representatives of the trade unions and the employers' organization *(Confindustria)*. The Commission did not succeed in reconciling the different views expressed and was therefore unable to produce a final consensus report. Despite its disagreement with the trade unions, the Government decided, in its finance bill, to propose the following changes to the method of calculating retirement pensions:

- a change in the percentage used to calculate the pension, the annual pension multiplier being reduced from 2 per cent to 1.75 per cent; and
- the introduction of a measure to reduce the seniority pension, in the case of early retirement, for each year between the actual date of retirement and the date when the person concerned reached retirement age. The reduction was fixed at 3 per cent.

The law provided for the immediate entry into force of these measures, without any transitional arrangements.

The intensity and the scale of the protests were such that the Government was forced to withdraw its measures and this undoubtedly had a crucial influence on its subsequent demise. However, the Berlusconi Government, in exchange for the withdrawal of its proposed measures, succeeded in obtaining a commitment by the trade unions to conclude an agreement, between then and June the following year, authorizing the Government to make the same savings as had been planned through the adoption of the measures that had been withdrawn. If the commitment was not fulfilled, the law allowed for the continuation of the freeze on seniority pensions which was scheduled to be lifted at the end of June 1995.

After the fall of the Berlusconi Government, due to the defection of the *Lega Nord*, a member of the centre-right coalition which had won the 1994 election, a centre-left Government, led by the President of the Council, Lamberto Dini, came to power. The Government was joined by the *Lega Nord,* whose programme included the reform of the compulsory pension system. It is probably worth mentioning that one of the reasons why the *Lega Nord* dissociated itself from the Berlusconi Government was undoubtedly the fact that its supporters included many industrial workers in the north of Italy, who were the primary beneficiaries of the pension system that Berlusconi was trying to abolish.

Unlike its predecessor, the Dini Government engaged in long and complex negotiations with the main trade unions and associations of the self-employed, and with the employers' organizations. The trade union representatives participated informally in each stage of the drafting of the Government bill.[14] At the start of the negotiations with all the economic and social representatives, the Government did not come forward with ready-made solutions. Its sole aim, at least on the surface, was to make the changes necessary to reduce the cost of financing the state pension system and, by a new method of calculating pensions, to achieve a better correlation between the contributions paid in and the benefits received by the insured. The main outlines of the new system were thus discussed and negotiated with all the parties concerned. This "dialogue" approach resulted, after long negotiations, in an agreement with the generality of social and economic representatives with the exception, albeit a significant one, of the main employers' organization (*Confindustria*). The agreement was officially signed in the office of the President of the Council on 8 May 1995.

It is important to note that the agreement was also signed by small trade unions and organizations representing the self-employed. While there is no doubt that this was the fruit of the dialogue approach adopted by the Government, it should nevertheless be underlined that the trade unions also had an objective interest in signing an agreement with a ruling coalition that was more sensitive to the difficulties of the workers' representatives. This sensitivity was essentially reflected in the granting of a long transition stage between the old pension system and the new one. For their part, the trade unions undertook gradually to persuade their members of the need to change the previous pension system, which was certainly more favourable. They were helped by the unusual circumstance, agreed at the joint launch of the reform, that the application of the new rules would be staged and that it would be done using sophisticated techniques. The government bill, which incorporated the terms of the agreement, was presented to Parliament, which passed it in August 1995 with a few minor amendments.

The Pension System Reform Act adopted in 1995 tried to fill a gap in the Italian institutional system, which did not provide for a special public body responsible for the supervision of the social security system, along the lines of the Social Security Board of Trustees in the United States or the British Social Security Advisory Committee. On the other hand, there was in Italy a public body in the Ministry of Finance, the Technical Committee on Public Expenditure, which had a more general duty to supervise public expenditure in the broad sense.[15]

One must not be under too many illusions that these bodies are in a position to contribute to achieving a consensus on the need to correct any imbalances in the pension system. They can, however, play a very useful role in stimulating debate between the parties concerned on the system's potential deficiencies or financial imbalances.

It was with this in mind that the 1995 reform act instituted a ministerial body, the Pension Costs Evaluation Unit (*Nucleo di Valutazione della Spesa Previdenziale*), to which it gave the job of monitoring and controlling the compulsory state pension system financed on a pay-as-you-go basis. The Unit's main tasks are to monitor:

- the activities of each pension scheme;
- the economic and financial development of the compulsory pension system;
- changes in the ratio of active members to pensioners; and
- income and expenditure, also for each pension scheme.

The Unit also has the more general task of monitoring and projecting the ratio of pension costs to GDP.

The law requires the results of the monitoring and the forecasts of financial equilibrium relating to the expenditure flows of each compulsory pension fund management institution to be communicated exclusively to the Ministry of Labour and Social Security, which in turn reports periodically to Parliament on the economic, financial and practical aspects of the 1995 pensions reform. The Unit's evaluations are thus published not directly, but through the Government and Parliament.

The progressive way in which the legislative changes take effect, and the simultaneous transition from the old to the new system of calculation, mean that the Unit's work is politically sensitive, since it is capable of leading to certain measures being taken. Moreover, the powerful inertia inherent in pension costs, and the slow and uncertain growth in economic activities and earned income which has led in recent years to serious stagnation in overall contributions, increase the likelihood that the Unit will come up with proposed adjustments to the current pension system. Although there is no express provision in the law, the Pension Costs Evaluation Unit itself decided, with the agreement of the Minister of Labour, who is responsible for it, to produce an annual report on the state of the public pension system. This report has, up to now, always been published.

With regard to voluntary complementary pensions financed by capitalization, which were introduced under the Amato reform and reinforced by the provisions of the Dini reform, the latter provided for the creation of a Pension Funds Supervisory Committee, responsible for supervising and controlling the activity of private institutions which manage this kind of complementary pension provision. The Commission's task, in particular, was to issue private funds with the authorizations to collect and administer employers' and employees' contributions, and to ensure sound management of the portfolios thus constituted.

In connection with possible corrections necessary to the pension system, the 1995 Reform Act included, for the short and medium term, two monitoring phases for which the technical responsibility was assigned to the Pension Costs Evaluation Unit:

- The first phase concerns possible adjustments needed during the first three years after the entry into force of the 1995 reform.
- The second phase begins at the end of the third year after the entry into force of the 1995 reform.

In the first phase, the monitoring is carried out a posteriori, at the end of each year and, where any divergences are noted from the amount of savings expected when the law was passed, the Government is authorized to make the necessary adjustments to restore the conditions necessary to achieve the financial targets, by adjusting benefits and contribution rates for as long as is necessary to achieve the intended results.

In the second phase, however, the Government is authorized to take action to protect and safeguard the proposed financial objectives, by taking measures based on income and expenditure projections prepared by the Unit for the next ten years.

In both cases, the law allows for automatic corrections, provided that they meet the prior conditions set out in the agreement with the social partners on making savings. Agreement on the objectives to be attained automatically leads on to agreement on the scale of measures to freeze the level of pensions that the Government may subsequently deem necessary. Only the most ambitious objectives of blocking pensions or qualitative changes in the existing system, such as the adjustments to the 1995 law adopted in 1997 by the Prodi Government, require the reopening of negotiations with the social partners.

Only two years after the law on reform of the pension system was passed, the Prodi Government, which can be regarded as fully in the political tradition of the Dini Government, even down to the method of dialogue, found itself in a situation which required a revision of the pension agreements concluded in 1995. This was essentially due to the accelerating process of convergence with the Maastricht parameters, which became clearly necessary in 1997 if Italy was to figure among the first group of countries participating in the launch of the euro. In order to justify to the public the restrictive measures that it was about to adopt for the pension system, the Prodi Government set up an expert commission – the Commission to Analyse the Macro-Economic Compatibility of Social Expenditure – early in 1997. Its members were nominated to the President of the Council, which seems to have been invested with broader powers, since it was mandated with presenting a proposal for the wholesale restructuring of the Italian Welfare State. The Commission concluded that the 1995 reform, while attaining the economic objectives that it had been set, had not, on the other hand, allowed stabilization of social expenditure in relation to GDP in the medium term. On the basis of these conclusions, and after the Commission had completed its work in March 1997, the Government launched a series of consultations with the social partners, and especially the trade unions, which continued until the end of September the same year. Compared with the ambitious programme of government reform, with the exception of the positive measures described above, the results of the negotiations were, in practice, very limited.

This can be explained by the trade unions' difficulty in accepting the new proposals for reform of the social security system, and not just pensions, which had been rejected by the New Communist Party (*Refondazione Comunista*). The latter was not a member of the Government, but supported it in Parliament where it gave it a majority. It is likely that if the government majority had been more coherent and had had autonomy in Parliament, the difficulties described above could have been overcome. In other words, the dialogue method encountered the resistance of a political force that saw itself as hostile while at the same time it constituted a crucial component of the numerical majority.

Conclusions

The model of economic, political and social relations which seems to have been imposed in Italy is based on dialogue. It tends to give responsibility to the social partners, especially workers' representatives. It is in the context of this general model, and its particular application to the pension field that a neutral and independent body (the Pension Costs Evaluation Unit) was set up, with the job of informing the parties to the agreement (i.e. the Government and the trade unions) of the results of the process of pension system reform, and to ensure that the two parties respected the terms of the agreement. In reality, because of the way it was set up and organized in practice, the Unit essentially reports to the Minister of Labour.

As we have seen, only two years after the conclusion of the 1995 agreement on pensions, the conditions requiring its revision were already present under the Prodi Government. If these conditions reoccurred, they put the dialogue approach at risk. Indeed, the trade unions, which were in danger of being forced to agree in advance to possible subsequent changes suggested by the second phase of monitoring the viability of the pension system (described above in connection with the Pension Costs Evaluation Unit), might have found themselves in a politically difficult position and might have been criticized for failing to represent their members.

One may wonder, therefore, whether the Prodi Government's approach aimed at amending the 1995 pension agreement only two years after it had been concluded was appropriate, bearing in mind the lack of homogeneity of views on the subject even within the ruling majority, which made it particularly difficult to obtain the cooperation of the trade unions.

The Italian experience seems to show that when one seeks to create the conditions necessary for a sharing of responsibility for the changes needed in the social security system in order to ensure its long-term macroeconomic viability, it is ultimately the wider political and economic conditions which determine the success or failure of these measures. And these conditions cannot be foreseen.

It is thus important that there is a body whose authority is beyond question with the social partners, which can define and "put on the negotiating table" the financial risks and problems of inequity within the pension system. One should not have too many illusions, however, that this would reduce social conflicts which, as the Italian experience shows, can be resolved by making the social partners responsible and engaging them in an organized and open process of dialogue. In this context, the trade unions must not be asked to accept or reject predetermined solutions which are closed to all debate. Of course, one cannot claim that the Government, in adopting this model, does not pay a certain price in the form of compromise solutions, a key feature of which is that they must be applied gradually in stages. Neither can one rule out trade unions' also paying a high price, even one that is unacceptable in the long term, given their function of representing the interests of workers and pensioners.

To sum up, the strengths of the Italian dialogue model seem to be the following:

- giving responsibility to the trade unions by making them face the same problems which the Government is called on to solve in the interest of society as a whole; and
- allowing the unions' consent to the introduction of changes to be obtained, even if these changes come in stages, while keeping social tensions to a low level.

The weaknesses of the model seem to be the following:

- the extreme progressive nature of the measures taken, a direct and clear consequence of the model;
- the obligation to constantly expose the pension system to small shocks, since the measures adopted cannot be radical in the short term;
- the lack of institutionalization of the model (except for certain aspects of law 335, described above), hence its lack of democratic transparency, a defect somewhat mitigated by the fact that in Italy laws proposed by the Government must always be debated in Parliament; and
- the fact that the Pension Costs Evaluation Unit is not in practice independent of the Government, since the law puts it under the direct authority of the Minister of Labour.

Notes

[1] As we shall see later, other changes were decided by the Ciampi Government (which succeeded the Amato Government), while the Berlusconi Government (which preceded the Dini Government) did not succeed in implementing its proposed reform.

[2] Assuming an increase in salaries based on an annual increase in GDP of 2 per cent.

[3] To be more precise, by its decree 373/1993, the Ciampi Government excluded from the calculation of the reference salary for pension entitlement, annual salaries lower than 80 per cent of the average salary received, taking into account a maximum of 25 per cent of working life (a limit which was raised for certain special categories such as journalists and pilots).

[4] Which reads as follows: "Any citizen unable to work and deprived of the essential means of daily life is entitled to be provided with subsistence expenses and social assistance. Workers are entitled to be protected and insured, by means appropriate to their fundamental needs, in case of accident, illness, disability and old age, involuntary unemployment … The organs and institutions of the State are charged with implementing the measures set out in this article."

[5] The need to translate the "social rights" set out in the Constitution into reality initially led to a progressive and general extension of the compulsory old-age pension scheme. Hence the following measures: compulsory insurance for categories of employees who, being in receipt of salaries in excess of those fixed by law for general compulsory insurance, had hitherto been exempt; the progressive extension of the same requirement, during 1959-66, to independent agricultural workers, farmers and farmworkers, artisans and traders, to the extent that they belonged to the least-protected categories of the self-employed; and the extension of different forms of compulsory social protection to certain categories of self-employed who had not yet been covered by compulsory insurance. Among the measures to implement the constitutional principles of protection by the social State, mention should be made of the minimum pension (law 118/1952), the creation of the Social Fund (law 903/1965) and the social pension (law 153/1969), the protection scheme for civilian disabled (law 118/1971) and, in the context of the introduction of a comprehensive social security system, the creation of the national health service (law 833/1978).

[6] These are essentially workers who are not under any form of subordination.

[7] This means the creation of a true pension system parallel to the existing one, bearing in mind the long transition period required, which is clearly much more than the usual notion of a transitional arrangement. It should be added that maintaining the old defined benefit system, for workers who had a contribution record of at least 18 years at 31 December 1995, gives rise to a structure comprising three associated pension systems: (a) new members (full application of the defined contribution system); (b) workers with a contribution record of less than 18 years at 31 December 1995 (application of the defined contribution system, with a system of pro rata calculation for the contribution years after that date); and (c) workers with a contribution record of over 18 years for whom, as already indicated, the defined benefit system continues to apply in full. The latter also have the option to transfer their pension in full to the defined contribution system.

[8] That is, maintaining the old pension scheme for pension contributions which had reached maturity.

[9] The fact that this revision may take place every ten years is one of the controversial points of the reform. Some argue that the conversion factors should evolve constantly in line with demographic changes, while others are worried about the effect of the new method on workers' willingness to retire, because of the defined time periods on which the amount of pension depends.

[10] In particular, the amount of the pension, under the defined contribution formula, is obtained by multiplying the individual notional amount accumulated by the worker, subject to a ceiling linked to the income concerned (equal to 139 million lira in 1998), by the conversion factor corresponding to the age of the insured at the date of retirement. The percentage of contribution for the calculation is fixed at 33 per cent. For benefits payable in the case of incapacity for work or disability benefits due to a worker who has not reached the age of 57 years, the conversion factor for age 57 is used. The same applies to pensions payable to survivors of a worker who dies in service before the age of 57. The percentage points of the conversion factor are increased as a function of age, according to the following progression: 57 years = 4,720; 58 years = 4,860; 59 years = 5,006; 60 years = 5,163; 61 years = 5,334; 62 years = 5,514; 63 years = 5,706; 64 years = 5,911; 65 years = 6,136.

[11] The defined benefit system favoured in particular young pensioners (via seniority pensions) who had had an "accelerated" career with much higher contributions in their final working years and the self-employed who obtained higher rates of return than their contributions would normally have allowed.

[12] Moreover, the number of cases to which this system would apply would be lower anyway, due to the raising of the minimum number of years and the age required to be entitled to a pension, the general obligation for all self-employed to have pension insurance and the more frequent use of the provision for preserving social security entitlements, to the extent that these factors ensure entitlement to a pension not less than the statutory minimum pension (which may also be on the basis of length of contribution record).

[13] It should, however, be noted in this respect that the principle of total equivalence between contributions paid and the percentage credited is not wholly guaranteed by the reform legislation. This means that there can be a gap either in the form of a real contribution percentage lower than that calculated (as in the case of the self-employed, even if, as we shall see, the 1997 Finance Act later reduced the gap to one percentage point, bringing the financing percentage down to 19 per cent, compared with 20 per cent under Law 335/95) or, conversely, in the form of a calculated percentage higher than the financing percentage – a situation attributable to the need to safeguard the financial stability of the fund management concerned.

[14] It is true that in the final stage of negotiations with the Government, the trade unions presented their own joint proposal for reform of the pension system, but this must be seen rather as a symbolic act for the benefit of their members, to mark their independence from the Government's proposal.

[15] In any event, it is to this Committee that we owe the first fully argued proposal which, from the end of the 1980s, recommended the Government to introduce urgent measures to correct expenditure on pensions.

The process of pension reform in Spain

8

Ana Maria Lagares Pérez*

Description of the social security system and current legislation

Created in 1963 under a framework law and described in greater detail in the general law on social security adopted in 1966, the Spanish social security system guarantees benefits to people within its scope (i.e. those engaged in an occupation) in the case of illness, temporary incapacity to work, disability, maternity and permanent incapacity, as well as pensions and family allowances. Membership is compulsory for all persons within its scope; membership is for life and for the whole system. From the time they start work, which brings them within the scope of all the various schemes in the system, employees and employers must pay contributions. This allows calculation of retirement pensions and pensions paid in respect of permanent incapacity, and of death and survivors' benefits, based on prior contribution periods. Thus the value of the pension paid at a given time is based on the calculation at that time. The State guarantees a minimum pension such that the necessary supplementary payments will be made to ensure that all pensions reach at least the minimum. The State also guarantees the purchasing power of pensions through an annual revaluation.

With regard to the contributory part, the system consists of a general scheme (for wage earners) and special schemes for the following: the agricultural sector, seafarers, self-employed, domestic servants, coalminers and students. The regulations for the general scheme serve as the reference for the special schemes, which tend to align their protection measures with it.

The fact that the 1978 Constitution made the creation of a universal state social security system mandatory rendered it necessary to adopt non-contributory forms of protection. Law No. 26 of 20 December 1990 allows the

---

* Social Security Department, International Labour Office.

award of old-age and disability pensions, and family allowances to Spanish citizens in need who do not normally have access to such benefits. Legally, these benefits are regarded as the beneficiaries' subjective rights, provided of course that they satisfy the required conditions. Their total amount is fixed each year in the general state budget and, for the moment, they are financed by a combination of social security contributions and state transfers.

Today, the various applicable laws, as well as other legal provisions at various levels which constitute the legal framework of the system, are consolidated in a single text: the general law on social security (Royal legislative decree of 20 June 1994, which approved the consolidated text[1] of the general law on social security) and related regulatory instruments.

The legislative process applicable to social security

In Spain, it is traditionally the central organs of the State that have had the role of legislating in the field of social security. They are also responsible for setting policy and supervising the system. The management and administration are generally assigned to government institutions.

The Ministry of Labour and Social Affairs is the central administrative State body responsible for proposing and implementing general government policies on labour, employment, social security and the social services. There are also a number of higher state bodies and, in addition to the Ministry, an under-secretariat, two general secretariats and the Secretariat of State for Social Security.

The Secretariat of State for Social Security directs and controls the public institutions responsible for management, deals with legal organization, prepares draft laws, and coordinates financial resources and expenditure. It is composed of the following departments:

1. Administration of Social Security (*Dirección General de Ordenación de la Seguridad Social*): this is a purely technical department whose work is assigned to officials of the social security administration grouped into different sections: lawyers, actuaries, statisticians, economists, financial controllers and accountants. These are established civil servants who have been appointed after passing various selection processes. The department is responsible for two types of task:
   • financial: establishment of income and expenditure accounts; drawing up of investment plans; control and monitoring of financial management and implementation of the budget; economic, financial and actuarial planning of social security;

- legal: drafting and organization of regulatory provisions; compilation and preparation of legal and case law studies; legal assistance related to social security.

2. Controller General of Social Security (*Intervención General de Ordenación de la Seguridad Social*): this is responsible for controlling the determination and payment of benefits, as well as the respect for financial obligations, with the implied consequences for revenue and expenditure, by means of audits and other checks. It also has the task of verifying the legality of collection of contributions, making investments and preparing financial statements, and it must report on budget proposals and investment plans.

The strong presence of the central organs of the State in Spanish social security legislation is evidenced by the large number of legislative instruments in which the law-making authority is not the only one concerned.

First, there is the framework law and various subordinate legislation. The framework law of 28 December 1963 (approved by the Franco Parliament of the time, the *Cortes*) consisted of two articles, the first of which contained the organizational structure of social security and the second a delegation of legislative power to the Government which, by decree of 21 April 1966, approved the consolidated text containing the principles of the framework law (known as the general law on social security). Law No. 24 of June 1972 on the financing and improvement of the protection provided by the central social security system (also approved by the *Cortes*) amended the law of 1966 using the same technique of delegation of legislative power, but this time to allow the Government to consolidate the legislation. The new democratic order had already been installed in Spain when Parliament approved Law No. 26 of 20 December 1990 on non-contributory benefits, which was both technical and administrative: on the one hand, it directly amended the wording of the general law on social security and, on the other, it delegated to the Government the power to prepare a consolidated text.

Secondly, in the case of contributory social security benefits, the various governments benefited from the delegation of legislative power and adopted two consolidated texts, one on 30 March 1974 (delegation by the law of 1972) and the current one, of 20 June 1994 (delegation by the law of 1990).

Thirdly, the executive power also produces legislation in the form of regulations, and the Ministry of Labour and Social Affairs is responsible for proposing such regulations in application of the law to the Government. The list of regulations adopted up to the present is a long one: the regulations cover all aspects of the law on social security, from membership and contributions to benefits.

Finally, the organization of social security has recently become the subject of other legal instruments outside the field of social security, such as the law on the budget and the Labour Code (*Estatuto de los Trabajadores*).

Role of public bodies involved in the review and reform of the social security system

The present social security system in Spain was created by the framework law on social security of 1963 and developed in the general law on social security of 1966. The latter unified the protection of the socially insured and mutual benefit societies (which existed before the civil war), opening the way to the final nationalization of social security, by preserving only in a very residual form the complementary schemes negotiated collectively as optional enhancements. Initially, then, the sources of law applicable to the social security system then in force reflected the predominant role of the State, bearing in mind the political regime that emerged from the Civil War. The first reforms to the above text were made in the same institutional context: the law on the improvement and financing of social security, promulgated in 1972, and the consolidated text of existing legislation, adopted in 1974.

For the social security system, the process of political transition in Spain involved the need to reconcile the political spirit of existing legislation, which was out of step with the new constitutional values (Spanish Constitution of 1978), to mitigate state control of social security and to create a trend towards pluralism of sources of production. These sources which, despite the state control, still predominate even today, could nevertheless enjoy a degree of collective autonomy.

It is certain that the current legislation clearly established the exclusive power of the State in the organization of social security by not allowing it to become the subject of a collective agreement, and without accepting any exception other than the creation of optional complementary schemes. Nevertheless, it is worth highlighting the very vigorous expressions of autonomy that emerged and that are reflected in the instruments of social dialogue through which, as we shall see in the next section, the major themes of social security were debated and negotiated, especially unemployment, retirement age, pensions, contributions, financing and so on. A distinction should be drawn, among these instruments of social dialogue, between those where the executive power, through the presence of its representatives, played a direct role (the Moncloa accords, the national agreement on employment, and the economic and social pact) – where negotiations involved state representatives in amending or reforming the legislation – and those in whose preparation the state representatives did not participate (the interconfederal framework agreement and the interconfederal agreement), but which merely presented proposals to the State, with a view to its taking decisions one way or the other.

Thus, it is due to the Moncloa accords, among others, that workers and employers participate in controlling and supervising the management of social security. The social security management institutions have, in addition to their management and administrative structures, tripartite bodies to control and monitor management: general councils and executive committees in each body (National Institute of Social Security, Treasury for Social Security, National Health Institute, Maritime Social Institute and National Employment Institute).

The general councils are responsible for establishing the criteria for the work of the institutes, preparing the budget and approving the annual report. They are composed of 13 members of the most representative trade unions elected on a proportional basis; 13 representatives of the most representative employers' organizations; and 13 representatives of the administration. They are required to meet in full session every three months, but they may also hold extraordinary meetings at the request of the chairperson or more than 20 per cent of their members.

The executive committees supervise and control the application of the agreements reached by the general council, and propose measures to improve the operation of the body concerned. They are composed of three trade union representatives, three employers' representatives and three from the administration, and meet in regular session every month.

The process of reform: From the Toledo Pact to the law of 15 July 1997 on consolidation and rationalization of the social security system

The unfolding of the process of reform of the social security system

The last major reform of Spanish social security took place within an existing legal framework which had been put in place, with difficulty, over many years. This had started (if we ignore much older texts) with the framework law of 1963 and the consolidated text of the general law on social security of 1966, mentioned above, as well as the subsequent reforms of 1972 and 1974.

Once the transition had begun, the Moncloa Pact put forward a number of changes, (described in the previous section). At that time there was an attempt to achieve consensual reform of social security. The 1978 reform, mentioned above, consisted mainly of the creation of bodies to manage social security, including an internal control and supervisory organ: the general council. The general councils brought the social security system closer to social and economic reality, and led to the opening of a debate among the social partners on the need for structural reforms.

The 1980s were marked by uncertainty over the viability of the system and a realization of the financial problems in social security (rising costs due to the ageing of the population and unemployment, while revenues were no longer sufficient because of the low levels of employment, the black economy, delays and fraud).

In 1981, on the occasion of the signing of the national agreement on employment, there was a first attempt at a social security pact between the Government and the social partners, aimed at a fundamental reform of the system. A parliamentary commission on reform was set up for the purpose, and although the pact was never signed, the commission constituted a kind of sounding-board which brought the problems to light. The discussions led to a first reduction in contributions and the promulgation of the general law on health and the law on pension plans and funds, which had an indirect impact on the social security system.

Later, in the context of Spain's entry into the European Community, the social and economic agreement of 1984 was negotiated, envisaging the creation of a commission on the reform of social security. As the work of the commission did not produce a result, the Government unilaterally introduced in Parliament a draft law which was adopted as Law No. 26 of 1985. The main objective of the law, on the one hand, was to establish a better balance and greater proportionality between the amount of contributions paid by insured persons and the level of benefits awarded and, on the other, to extend the contribution periods required to be entitled to benefits and used to determine the amount of the pension.

Law No. 26 of 1985 did not gain any social support. It was considered inadequate in employers' circles and was firmly rejected by the trade unions. Just after its entry into force, the trade union Workers' Committees (*Comisiones Obreras*, CC.OO) called a strike, the first since the restoration of democracy in Spain.

The various amendments to the legislation rapidly proved incomplete, and were followed by other draft amendments, all equally ill received by the social partners. The Government's initiatives were all firmly rejected by the trade unions, to the extent that they led to the general strike of 14 December 1988. In an attempt to satisfy, if only in part, the trade union demands concerning what was then called the "social debt,"[2] Parliament adopted a number of measures, albeit of very limited scope.

The high rates of economic growth experienced by Spain in the 1980s and 1990s alleviated the financial imbalances and damped down the crisis that was threatening the social security system. However, massive job losses and a slowdown in the economy forced all sectors to shoulder their responsibilities and attempt to set up a viable social security system. As the state of the system's budget began to cause concern, the Congress of Deputies, in full session, approved a resolution on 15 February 1994 to set up a special working group. This had the task of preparing a report analysing the structural problems in the social security system and suggesting the main reforms that should be made during the next few years to secure the future of the state pension scheme and avoid large deficits in the national budget. The report was also to include recommendations to the Government. Decisions and structural reforms relating to the pension scheme would be based on this report.

The working group was formed on 2 March 1994, within the Parliamentary Budgetary Committee. It was composed of representatives of the following political groups: socialist, popular, joint, Canaries, United Left–Catalan Left (IU–IC) and the Basque Nationalist Party (PNV).[3] The group began by interviewing senior civil servants and experts, starting on 22 March 1994 and finishing on 27 September of the same year. It then appeared to be in an impasse for a while, until the chairperson of the Budgetary Committee revived the work by calling a meeting in Toledo (a city near Madrid).

In February 1995, the working group managed to reach an agreement which took the name "Toledo Pact", the full name being "Draft report prepared by the Working Group on the Analysis of the Social Security System and the principal reforms that should be carried out". The agreement was political in nature, and aimed to prevent social security becoming permanently embroiled in financial difficulties and used as a political pawn by the political parties, especially during elections.

The main objective of the Toledo Pact was to consolidate the social security model without giving up the fundamental framework laid down since 1966, by embarking on progressive reform, especially in the field of pensions. To this end, the Pact proposed to confirm the validity of the pay-as-you-go system as against the capitalization system, to differentiate between sources of financing (contributions and taxation), to align the contribution base to real wages and to emphasize control over benefits (especially in the case of temporary incapacity).

This first, political step – the Toledo Pact – was followed by a second, which was social as well as political in nature: the consolidation agreement of 9 October 1996, signed by the Head of the present Government and the general secretaries of the two main trade unions, the CC.OO and the General Workers' Union (UGT), but not the employers, who had reservations about the financial viability of the Toledo Pact. This agreement, which will remain in force until the year 2000, resulted in renewed dialogue between the Government and the trade unions with the goal, essentially, of maintaining pensioners' purchasing power and ensuring the financial stability of the social security system.

The final step towards a complete reform of the social security system was the adoption of Law No. 24 of 1997 on the consolidation and rationalization of the social security system. This is an excellent example of a negotiated legislative instrument since, before being debated and adopted in Parliament, its content was widely discussed by the Government with the trade unions, and was in fact the translation into law of the Toledo Pact and the agreement on pensions concluded with the trade unions.

Translation of the Toledo Pact and the consolidation agreement into the Law of 15 July 1997 on the consolidation and rationalization of the social security system

The content of the Toledo Pact, the consolidation agreement concluded with the trade unions and Law No. 24 of 1997 are far from simple, but can be summarized on the basis of three fundamental issues: (a) financial reform of the system; (b) pension reform; and (c) ways of improving the management of the system.

1. Financial reform of the system

In the case of the financial reform of the system, the first question addressed by the instruments is the definitive separation and clarification of the sources of social security financing, the second the establishment of rules for constituting reserves, and the third, financing of special schemes.

Concerning the differentiation of sources of financing, the first recommendation of the Toledo Pact was that contributory benefits should be financed essentially by social contributions (this formula leaves the way open for topping up by budget transfers where contributions are insufficient) and universal, non-contributory benefits exclusively from taxation.

The consolidation agreement developed the content of this recommendation by adding details of each benefit and specifying the type of financing applicable. Contributory benefits, in broad terms, were cash benefits and those paid in the event of industrial injury or occupational disease, as were the related expenses. They were to be financed from contributions. But it was also necessary to use other revenues, such as those from fines, surcharges and investment income related to social security. Non-contributory benefits and complementary benefits designed to guarantee a minimum pension (minimum complementary benefits) were to be financed from taxation. Law No. 24 of 1997 faithfully reflects the provisions of the agreement and provides for a progressive separation of the sources of social security financing up to the financial year 2000, in terms to be set each year by the General State Finance Act. It further provides that, in the meanwhile, the precise legal nature of the minimum complementary benefits should be decided, and that these benefits would be determined each year under the general State Finance Act.

Another aspect that should be taken into account in the diversification of social security financing was included in the second recommendation of the Toledo Pact. This was a proposal aimed at stabilizing the system without the need to increase contributions, by establishing a reserve fund financed by contribution surpluses in each budget year. As Law No. 24 of 1997 states, the reserve fund must be constituted in a way that takes account of progress towards separation of sources of financing. In the year 2000, it will be possible to judge whether the reserve fund is sufficient, based on the relevant actuarial calculations.

With regard to the deficit position of some special schemes (the agricultural sector scheme and the domestic servants' scheme), which has a negative impact on the general scheme, the Toledo Pact proposes to pay benefits proportional to the contributions collected and to reduce the number of such schemes to two (the self-employed scheme and the employees' scheme).

The agreement stresses the need to simplify the special schemes and questions the practice of using the surpluses of some schemes to cover the deficits of others. Law No. 24 of 1997 takes the same approach and authorizes the Government to carry out, within eight months, a study into the reduction of the number of special schemes.

2. Reform of the pension scheme

The second important aspect of restoring the financial position of the social security system, on which the Toledo Pact, the consolidation agreement and Law No. 24 of 1997 propose a number of measures, consists of the following points:

- the progressive alignment of the contribution base and real wages, until there is a single ceiling which will be based on movements in the consumer price index (CPI) and fixed by law;
- the proportionality between benefits and contributions. The consolidation agreement and Law No. 24 of 1997 developed the content of the Toledo Pact and decided on a progressive increase in the number of years (eight) taken as the basis for the calculation of the average salary up to 15 by the year 2001;
- to maintain pensioners' purchasing power, the Toledo Pact envisaged the automatic revaluation of benefits based on the CPI. The consolidation agreement provided that review clauses should be included for the financial year in cases where the actual CPI was higher than that forecast. Law No. 24 of 1997 not only incorporated the foregoing, but enhanced the provisions of the agreement by proposing an alternative: if actual CPI is higher than forecast, the difference must be paid to the pensioner as a lump sum; if the reverse is true, the difference in favour of the social security system must be absorbed in subsequent pension reviews.

3. Improved management

Lastly, the three instruments contain various measures aimed at improving the management of the system, including fraud prevention.

Conclusions

The successive reforms of the Spanish social security system since its creation in 1963 have all tried to link the wishes of the State to those of the social partners, especially since the political change which led to a new system of government. The goal of this spirit of conciliation was to develop existing legislation into the social state model defined by the Constitution of 1978, reflecting the changes in Spanish society following the death of Franco.

In one way or another, the spirit of tripartism (State, trade unions, employers) has been a constant feature of the process of reform. The desire to make changes to the system with the maximum of agreement between the country's political and social actors was a prime objective of all governments in the democratic period. This conciliatory spirit became a reality with the Toledo Pact.

The Toledo Pact and the consolidation agreement (with the guarantee of stability provided by the adoption of Law No. 24 of 1997, which incorporates and fixes their principles) are landmarks at a time when there is a need to decide on measures to overcome the weaknesses in the system. In so doing, one must not lose sight of the fact that the objective is, on the one hand, to prevent any reduction or erosion of the levels of coverage corresponding to needs and on the other, to satisfy a number of requirements such as maintaining the purchasing power of pensions.

In this respect, the 1998 social security budget (the first since approval of the reform) is a model of social protection which consolidates the reforms already introduced, but reconciles austerity and strict control of costs with an improvement in social welfare, so as to meet the expected increase in the costs of social protection, along the lines recommended by the Toledo Pact.

Although the process of total separation of sources of financing is scheduled to extend to the year 2000, the 1998 budget already introduced the changes aimed at increasing State participation in the financing of costs which were previously part of the social security budget (certain health costs, for example). It firmly established the automatic revaluation of contributory pensions, thus implementing the terms of Law No. 24 of 1997. The 1998 budget also guaranteed minimum pensions, suitably updated in line with CPI forecasts, and contained various measures to combat fraud, illicit benefit claims and arrears of contribution payments.

In conclusion, it must be said that the financing of the social security system is much clearer as a result of the Toledo Pact and the law on the consolidation and rationalization of the system. The process now under way of separating sources of financing and improving the situation relating to job creation, which can at last be observed in Spain, are reasons for thinking that the reform is now on the right track.

Notes

[1] The consolidated text is the result of delegation of legislative authority by Parliament. Parliament delegates to the Government a task of a technical, non-legislative nature: to consolidate a number of laws on the same subject in a single law without altering the provisions contained in those laws.

[2] A name which, in political circles, was given to the entirety of points needing reform in the social security system that were regarded as fundamental.

[3] These are all the political groups represented in Parliament.